Early Modern England

An Enthralling Overview of the Tudors, Stuarts, Renaissance, Reformation, and Other Events That Shaped Early Modern England

Table of Contents

INTRODUCTION 1
CHAPTER 1: WHO WERE THE TUDORS? 4
CHAPTER 2: WHO WERE THE STUARTS? 13
CHAPTER 3: THE MONARCHY IN EARLY MODERN ENGLAND 21
CHAPTER 4: KEY ENGLISH FIGURES FROM 1485 TO 1714 39
CHAPTER 5: THE RENAISSANCE 49
CHAPTER 6: THE REFORMATION AND HENRY VIII 60
CHAPTER 7: EXPLORATION AND TRADE 70
CHAPTER 8: PROTESTANTISM AND ITS GROWTH 77
CHAPTER 9: LAW(S) AND ORDER 86
CHAPTER 10: REVOLUTION AND REBELLION 95
CHAPTER 11: SOCIETAL STRUCTURE 106
CHAPTER 12: BATTLES AND WARS ABROAD 114
CHAPTER 13: SCOTLAND AND WALES 123
CHAPTER 14: THE IRISH QUESTION 133
CHAPTER 15: CONQUEST AND COLONIZATION 144
CHAPTER 16: THE CONTINUATION OF THE EMPIRE 152

CONCLUSION	162
HERE'S ANOTHER BOOK BY ENTHRALLING HISTORY THAT YOU MIGHT LIKE	165
FREE LIMITED TIME BONUS	166
BIBLIOGRAPHY	167

Introduction

Early modern England.

The name itself suggests some sort of progress. The word "modern" makes us think of this period as the first step in the process of development that would eventually transform England into the modern society of today. But how true is that?

The idea that there is some sort of sharp divide between the Middle Ages and the early modern era is fiction. The Battle of Bosworth in 1485 saw the end of the Plantagenet dynasty and the start of the Tudors, but the change in ruling dynasties did not automatically end medieval society. The transformation of a nation is a much slower process than that.

Instead of seeing early modern England as the absolute end of medieval society and the hard beginning of modern society, it can be helpful to view this entire period as a time of transition. This was a connecting period that led England from the Middle Ages into the modern era, but it took over two hundred years to do that.

In this book, you'll learn about the gradual changes that took place in English society from 1485 to 1714 and how those changes led to the modern England we know today. Everything from economics to religion to government was changing during this time, but those changes took decades, and the journey was not the strictly uphill climb that we like to picture. Real history is far more complicated than that.

For instance, did you know that witch trials took place in this era but not in the Middle Ages? So much for the idea that it was just medieval law that could be ignorant and cruel. Also, Shakespeare, that pretentious guy that everyone had to read in school, was not particularly sophisticated. His plays entertained the public and were considered by some to be scandalous. This was indeed the age of the Renaissance, but it wasn't all enlightened thinking and high-class art.

Then there is the matter of England's empire. England would begin to build its colonial empire in this period, greatly increasing its wealth and influence. The colonization of the New World connected the world to a previously unimagined extent, but there were also a lot of dark sides to this expansion. Natives, African slaves, and even indentured servants from England were treated horribly and lost their lives for the sake of the empire's progress.

Another example of complicated changes is religion. The Reformation saw the introduction of many new denominations of Christianity, which we put under one label of Protestantism. Over time, so many different religious opinions forced religious tolerance, but it took quite a long time to get there. In the immediate aftermath (and by immediate, we mean for the next two hundred years or so) of the Reformation, religious tolerance was seen as a bad thing. Many people were killed, discriminatory laws were passed, and even full-scale revolutions occurred because of an extreme lack of religious tolerance.

So, if you think that early modern England was a time when England was walking into the light and out of the "darkness" of the Middle Ages, think again. History of any time and any place involves change, but that change is rarely just good or bad. As you read about this era, remember that this is not the story of inevitable human progress. This is the story of a real nation and real people. England made some advancements during this period, but there are also some low points and other things that are neither good nor bad.

Is early modern England a fitting name, or is it a deceptive title designed to make us think that this period was more progressive than it really was? It depends. What do you consider to be a mark of modern society? Is it more personal freedom, a bureaucratic government, a more economically connected world, a less agricultural-based society, or something else? As you read about various events and trends in this era, consider what you think modernity is and whether you can see the roots of that in early modern England. Either way, you are bound to discover something you didn't know about the period from 1485 to 1714 in English history.

Chapter 1: Who Were the Tudors?

Dividing history into eras is both beneficial and tricky. Looking at a particular era, like early modern England, gives us a much more manageable chunk of information to explore, but it immediately raises the question of boundaries. If we want to talk about early modern England, where do we start, and where do we end? We'll save the second question for much later in the book, but we have to figure out where we should start before we can even begin to explore this unique and interesting time.

Roughly, early modern England encompassed the 15th to the 18th century. However, "roughly" isn't quite good enough. If we are just using rough dates, then events taking place in the transition between periods become hard to define. Are the Wars of the Roses part of early modern England just because they took place in the 15th century? Most people tend to consider this a medieval event. To avoid this type of confusion, historians tend to draw lines in the sand when they divide history into different periods. A particular event is used to mark the end of one age and the beginning of another.

In many ways, setting these strict dates is misleading. The transition between these periods is often the result of gradual change rather than a singular event. However, singular events give us clear boundaries to organize our history and watershed moments that vividly illustrate the changing times. In a monarchy like England, there is an almost built-in system for defining different eras. The reigns of various monarchs have often been used to define periods in English history, such as the Elizabethan era and the Victorian era, and it is this system that we typically use to define the early modern era. Medieval England fell with the Plantagenet dynasty, and early modern England rose with the Tudors.

Who Were the Tudors?

For us and early modern England, the watershed moment was 1485. The place was Bosworth. After decades of internal fighting in the Wars of the Roses, England was under the control of Richard III, who was rumored to have murdered his nephews to secure the throne for himself. The Houses of Lancaster and York had almost annihilated each other in their rivalry for the throne, and it seemed that Richard III, who was of the House of York, was simply the last man standing. However, there was one remaining claimant on the Lancastrian side: Henry Tudor.

If you are wondering just who Henry Tudor is, you aren't far off from what many people of the day might have thought. Henry Tudor had a dubious claim to the English throne at best. He was the son of Edmund Tudor and Margaret Beaufort. Margaret Beaufort was the great-granddaughter of John of Gaunt, who started the House of Lancaster and was Edward III's son. Edmund Tudor was the son of Catherine of Valois, Henry V's widow, and a Welshman by the name of Owen Tudor. Edmund Tudor was the half-brother of Henry VI, the last true Lancastrian king. Thus, Henry Tudor could claim the throne through both his mother's and his father's side.

If it sounds confusing, don't worry; it is. No one believed Henry Tudor had a strong claim to the throne, but by 1485, it didn't really matter that much. Everyone with a better claim was dead. Henry Tudor was the sole surviving member of the Lancastrian side, and he decided to try to take the throne from Richard III. In 1485, the two forces met at Bosworth. Richard III was a veteran hardened by the Wars of the Roses, and Henry Tudor was a young man with little experience. Had it been a one-on-one duel, there is no doubt who would have walked away, but luckily for Henry, it wasn't. Henry's forces were victorious, and Richard III died during the battle. Henry Tudor was soon crowned Henry VII.

Richard III at the Battle of Bosworth by James William Edmund Doyle.
https://commons.wikimedia.org/wiki/File:A_Chronicle_of_England_-_Page_453_-_Richard_III_at_Bosworth.jpg

With Henry's victory at Bosworth and Richard III's death, England saw not just a change of kings but also a change of dynasties. Richard III was the last of the Plantagenets, a line that had ruled England for over three hundred years. Henry Tudor began a new line that would lead England through the Reformation and the Renaissance. The Tudors may have been a relatively unknown Welsh family at first, but they would become one of England's most successful and famous ruling families.

The Tudor Myth

Beginning with Henry VII in 1485 and ending with the death of Elizabeth I in 1603, the Tudors ruled England for 118 years. They began their reign at the end of the Wars of the Roses when England was emerging from the Middle Ages, and the Tudors used the timing of their reign to their advantage.

If you think that modern political figures are the only ones who worry about image, think again. Even back in 1485, rulers were constantly concerned with the overall myth that surrounded them. Propaganda was not a tool invented in the 20th century, but it did look a bit different during the time of the Tudors. To be the monarch was to be more than a person. It was to be a symbol, and the Tudors understood that perhaps better than any dynasty that ruled before them.

So, what exactly did the Tudors do? During the Tudor era, the Middle Ages was consistently painted as the Dark Ages. The medieval period was seen as a time of ignorance, violence, and stagnation. Portraying the period that came before their rule in such a horrible light made it easy for the Tudors to portray their own rule as a golden age. They were the rulers who saved England from the muck of the Dark Ages and ushered it into a time of prosperity.

The fact that many people still think of the Middle Ages as the Dark Ages shows just how effective the Tudors were at perpetuating this myth. But how exactly did they manage it?

The symbol that Henry VII took after he became king is a prime example of how this worked. Henry VII took the Tudor rose as his symbol, which is a white and red rose.

Tudor rose.
Sodacan This W3C-unspecified vector image was created with Inkscape., CC BY-SA 3.0 <https://creativecommons.org/licenses/by-sa/3.0>, via Wikimedia Commons: https://commons.wikimedia.org/wiki/File:Tudor_Rose.svg

This two-hued rose served as a symbol for the union of the Houses of York and Lancaster, whose conflict had caused the very bloody Wars of the Roses. By picking the white and red rose as his symbol, Henry VII constantly reminded everyone that he was the one who had brought an end to the civil war and restored peace to England. It was a brilliant political move, but how accurate was this symbolism?

The short answer is not nearly as much as we want it to be. The red and white Tudor rose works because it combines the red rose of the Lancasters and the white rose of the Yorks. The only problem is that the two houses didn't use the rose symbols prominently. Both sides had multiple families and multiple standards and heralds. During the Wars of the Roses, the two opposing sides were not facing off under different colored rose banners.

So, why is it called the Wars of the Roses then? Simply put, the Tudors were incredibly successful at rewriting history. Henry VII's Tudor rose, even with its dubious origins, was a powerful symbol. When people in the Tudor era looked back at the chaotic civil war of the 15th century, they applied the symbol they knew to it, and the conflict soon became the Wars of the Roses. Thanks to Shakespeare immortalizing this idea in his play *Henry VI, Part 1*, the idea that each side was represented by a different colored rose has become so prevalent that most people think it's real history.

The Tudor rose is just one small aspect of the Tudor myth. The Tudor era also saw the great vilification of Richard III. Henry VII was technically a conquering king. He won his throne on the field of battle, so to make the Tudor claim more legitimate and avoid being styled as a usurper, it was important that the king from whom Henry VII had taken the throne was seen in the worst possible light.

Again, we know that the Tudors were very successful here because history does not remember Richard III kindly. Shakespeare portrayed him as a hunchbacked tyrant who was so power-hungry that he murdered his own nephews for the crown. Who wouldn't prefer the golden rule of the Tudors to someone like that? By painting Richard III as the worst possible villain (being dead, he couldn't do much to defend himself), Henry VII and his successors furthered the idea that they were the saviors of England.

So, that's the Tudor myth. It's the idea that the Middle Ages was a truly dark time and that the Tudors were the ones who brought England out of this darkness and into the light. But why is the Tudor myth important? For one, it was so effective that it has greatly influenced the way we understand both Tudor England and medieval England to this day. We still call it the Wars of the Roses, Richard III is still considered one of England's worst kings, the medieval period is still called the Dark Ages, and Tudor England is still a golden age in English history.

Knowing about the Tudor myth is important as we dive deeper into this era of English history. Some of your preconceptions about this time may be challenged. While England did see a lot of progress and growth during the Tudor era, it was not a completely golden age any more than the medieval period was a total dark age.

What Was Tudor England Really Like?

Now that we have taken a look at why the Tudor age tends to be a bit overly glorified in English history, let's consider what the period from 1485 to 1603 was really like. Is there any truth to the idea that this was England's golden age?

Like most effective myths, the Tudor myth works because there is some truth to it. The Tudor era saw a lot of changes for England, and many of those changes allowed England to transform into a world power that, by 1922, had an empire that spread across a quarter of the globe.

The event that captures this change the most succinctly is the defeat of the Spanish Armada by the English in 1588 during Elizabeth I's reign. When the Spanish fleet tried to cross the English Channel to invade England, they were defeated by the English navy, with the Spanish fleet returning home in shambles. We will discuss the details of this immense English victory in Chapter 12, but for now, let's consider why this event was so important and what it tells us about England under the Tudors.

Defeating the Spanish Armada was the moment at which the

English took command of the seas. The naval dominance that England won in 1588 would be maintained for the next several centuries and is one of the biggest factors that allowed Britain to become a world power. During the coming times of colonization and trade, England's control of the waves gave them a distinct advantage. If the English had not destroyed the Spanish fleet in 1588, Britain likely would not have become the world's leading colonizing power in the next few centuries.

So, the defeat of the Spanish Armada was crucial for establishing Britain's naval preeminence, but how much does it tell us about Tudor England? This important victory against a foreign power hints at something perhaps even more important about the Tudors. They maintained internal stability.

Although history has exaggerated things to some degree, medieval England was indeed a violent and sometimes chaotic place. There were two civil wars (the Anarchy and the Wars of the Roses), which resulted in the breakdown of basic law and order, and many other smaller internal conflicts. Fighting amongst themselves to such an extent left the English with little time to make an impact on a global scale in the Middle Ages. However, under the Tudors, the monarchy stabilized.

Although religious tensions ran high during the Tudor era, they never erupted into a full-scale war. In some ways, the Tudor era was a golden age simply because England didn't have any major internal conflicts. One hundred eighteen years under a single ruling family without a major internal dispute created a more united England, one that could stand strong against other foreign powers. The defeat of the Spanish Armada is thus not only significant for its impact on England's future but also in showing how much England had healed under the Tudors. The war-ravaged land of 1485 would never have been able to defeat Europe's leading power, but one hundred years of relative stability under the Tudors had created a far more powerful nation.

Wait. Does that mean the Tudor era was a golden age? Not quite. One major misunderstanding that the Tudor myth has caused about this era is the assumption that it was far more progressive than the Middle Ages. The Tudor era was the time of Shakespeare and the Renaissance. It was a time when trade was expanding, and England was getting richer. However, that is only telling part of the story. In many areas, there is not as much of a sharp divide between medieval and early modern England as the Tudor myth has taught us to believe.

For example, one of the main reasons that Tudor England did not see a major internal conflict was because of how harshly the germs of rebellions were stifled. Revolts like the Pilgrimage of Grace, the Prayer Book Rebellion, and Kett's Rebellion were crushed swiftly and thoroughly. Although trade expanded and feudalism ended, Tudor England saw an increase in poverty, and the strict divide between the social classes remained. This era saw the expansion of schools and education, but it also saw a sudden spike in trying women for witchcraft. There were great discoveries made thanks to exploration, but there was also the rise of piracy and the slave trade.

So, while Tudor England did see many advancements, it was not a purely golden age. No era in history is. It was a time of change, but it was not a time of pure progress. The Tudor myth is just that, a myth.

The Legacy of Tudor England

Even so, the Tudors did forever change England. The period from 1485 to 1603 was crucial in transforming England into a nation in the modern sense of the word.

In the medieval period, the country's structure was based on the feudal system. This hierarchal structure had each noble ruling over his land and answering to the king only when necessary, usually in times of war. It was a pyramid in which the king, and hence the central government, was at the top. This meant the central government had direct control over relatively little.

During the Tudor era, the central government's power grew. Instead of every noble being the king of his own small kingdom on his country estate, the country's ruling elite spent more time in London in government positions. Parliament passed more acts, and the government was far more involved in the economy. The English government was transforming from a pyramid structure to a tree where the trunk of the central government branched out to various sub-sections.

This transformation of governing styles was essential if England was to thrive in the early modern world. The nation had to be able to act with a unified sense of identity and interest in the competitive economic realities of the 16th century. The Tudors helped make this possible by expanding the monarchy to represent more than just them. The monarch was no longer just a person. They were the embodiment of England. The reality behind that ideal was an ever-growing bureaucratic system that served the nation's increasingly complex governmental needs.

However, this expansion of the central government would not come without its challenges. What would happen when the monarch and the governing class disagreed? England's next ruling dynasty would have to answer that question.

Chapter 2: Who Were the Stuarts?

Elizabeth I is one of England's most well-remembered monarchs. She ruled long enough to have an entire era named after her, and the nation prospered under her. She was a well-liked monarch, but she did have one rather annoying flaw. She refused to name an heir.

We will talk more about Elizabeth I, but if you don't already know, Elizabeth I was famous for being the Virgin Queen. She never married, ruling England as the sole monarch for close to forty-five years. Obviously, that meant she did not have any direct heirs because she had no children. Perhaps that would not have been such a problem, but Elizabeth I also seemed to think she was going to live forever. No matter how her advisers prodded her, Elizabeth I would not name her successor.

Was Elizabeth I just being unreasonably stubborn? To a degree, yes, but she did have a reason. The English court was a solar system, and everyone orbited around the monarch. The closer you were to the queen or king, the more power you had. When Elizabeth I named an heir, she would essentially be creating a secondary solar system. People, especially those who were unhappy with Elizabeth, would begin flocking to the future monarch to try to gain favor in anticipation of Elizabeth's death. If Elizabeth named a successor, she might very well be pushing her opponents and maybe even supporters into the arms of a powerful rival.

Thus, Elizabeth I refused to name an heir. However, she was mortal, and the day came when the queen died.

The Stuarts

In 1603, Elizabeth I died, and while she may have put off the matter during her lifetime, the throne had to pass to someone. Unclear succession was a dangerous thing in a monarchy. In England's past, it had led to a long and bloody civil war. No one wanted to see that happen again, which is why when Elizabeth I died, her advisers already had the next man picked: James Stuart, or rather James VI of Scotland.

James I by John de Critz.
https://commons.wikimedia.org/wiki/File:James_I,_VI_by_John_de_Critz,_c.1606.png

In some ways, James Stuart was the obvious pick because he was Elizabeth I's closest relative of royal blood. To understand just who

James was, we have to go back to the first Tudor king: Henry VII. Henry VII had four children: Arthur, Henry, Margaret, and Mary. Arthur died young before he had any children. While Henry VIII was famous for having many wives, he only had three children, all of whom died without children to take the throne. Since family names were only passed through the male line, the Tudor line died with the last of Henry VIII's children, Elizabeth I.

However, while the Tudors were gone, that did not mean there was no one left who carried Henry VII's blood. His daughter and third child, Margaret, married James IV of Scotland. Their granddaughter was Mary, Queen of Scots (there were several important figures named Mary at this time, so to avoid confusion, this Mary is always referred to as Mary, Queen of Scots). Mary, Queen of Scots was Elizabeth I's cousin and closest blood relative before her death in 1587. After Mary, Queen of Scots died, her son, James Stuart, became the English queen's closest relative.

James Stuart had the best blood claim to the throne, but his succession was by no means certain. Elizabeth and James's mother had not gotten along. In fact, Elizabeth I had Mary, Queen of Scots executed for her involvement in a plot against the Crown. It was unclear if James's mother's treason would prohibit him from inheriting the throne.

There was also the matter of James being Scottish. James Stuart was better known as James VI of Scotland. He had been the king of Scotland since his mother was forced to abdicate in 1567. Scotland and England had a less than friendly history as well as different churches by this point (Scotland was Presbyterian, and England was Anglican). Would the English accept a Scottish king?

To much surprise and relief, James Stuart's ascension to the throne of England went smoothly. It may be that his previous experience as a monarch made the English more willing to accept him, or perhaps they simply preferred any king that ascended peacefully over the chaos of having several people vie for the crown. Either way, in 1603, James VI of Scotland became James I of England, and the line of Stuart monarchs began. The Stuarts would rule England for the next 111 years, with a significant eleven-year gap in the middle of that period.

You might think that with James Stuart being both James VI of Scotland and James I of England that Scotland would be united with England and Wales to form the country of Great Britain. Surprisingly, that union was still one hundred years away. Although they shared a monarch, Scotland and England still had separate parliaments and separate governments. James Stuart was James VI of Scotland and James I of England at the same time.

England under the Stuarts

England under the Tudors is seen as a golden age in English history, but no one says the same thing about England under the Stuarts.

Royal arms of the Stuarts.
Sodacan This W3C-unspecified vector image was created with Inkscape., CC BY-SA 3.0 < https://creativecommons.org/licenses/by-sa/3.0>, via Wikimedia Commons: https://commons.wikimedia.org/wiki/File:Royal_Arms_of_England_(1603-1707).svg

The Stuart dynasty ruled England for 111 years, from 1603 to 1714. During that time, two Stuart monarchs were ousted. One was executed, and the other fled the country. There was a nine-year civil war. The capital city nearly burned to the ground in the Great Fire of 1666, and England was involved in many costly wars with foreign powers. What went wrong? What happened to the growth of the Tudor era?

The first thing we should clarify is that the Stuart era was not a dark age any more than the Tudor era was a golden one. There were a lot of noticeable problems in this era, but by the end of it, England was well on its way to becoming one of the world's most powerful nations. The growth of the Tudor era did continue, especially in the economy. What the Tudor era had that the Stuart era lacked was internal peace.

What went wrong with the Stuarts was in part a result of the governmental growth that occurred under the Tudors. When James I became the first Stuart monarch of England, the English government was long past the stage where the monarch could effectively rule without Parliament's consent, but this system of cooperation between monarch and Parliament was at odds with the Stuarts' understanding of the monarchy. Monarchs like James I and Charles I believed strongly in the king's sovereignty. They would not play the game of negotiating with Parliament, and the tensions this caused eventually erupted into the English Civil War.

This does not mean that the Tudors ran England as a constitutional monarchy or that the early Stuarts were tyrants. Tudor monarchs were absolute monarchs, but where Henry VIII and Elizabeth I succeeded and James I and Charles I failed was public relations. The Tudors knew how to sell themselves. In Elizabeth's addresses to Parliament, she was sure of her own power but also tactful.

For example, in a speech shortly after she ascended the throne, Elizabeth I said, "The burden that is fallen upon me maketh me amazed, and yet considering I am God's creature, ordained to obey his appointment, I will thereto yield." Calling the throne a "burden" was Elizabeth leaning into the perceived limitations of her sex, but she quickly flips this by saying that she has been appointed by God and therefore must yield to the appointment. She is claiming that she has divine approval but in a disarmingly humble way.

Charles I was not as tactful with his dealings with Parliament. In a speech in 1641, shortly before tensions between the king and Parliament erupted into civil war, Charles I said, "Nay, I have given way to every thing that you have asked of me, and therefore me thinkes you should not wonder if in some thing I begin to refuse, but I hope it shall not hinder your Progresse in your great Affaires. And I will not sticke upon triviall matters to give you Content, I hope you are sensible of these beneficiall favours bestowed upon you at this time."

Here, Charles I is informing an already greatly disgruntled Parliament that they ought to be grateful for what he has done for them. You can almost hear the sarcasm behind phrases like "I hope it shall not hinder *your* progress in *your* great affairs" and "I hope *you* are sensible of these beneficial favors bestowed upon you at this time." This was not the way to deal with Parliament. They had had too much real power for far too long to take such an overbearing attitude from the monarch.

Charles I was the only monarch to lose his head, but he wasn't the only Stuart monarch to lose the throne. Charles I's son, James II, had to flee the country after his own people invited William of Orange to invade. What did James II do that was so horrible? He committed the ultimate sin in the eyes of the English people in the 17th century. He was Roman Catholic.

The overthrow of Charles I and James II shows us the paradoxical nature of England in the Stuart era. On the one hand, this was a time when notions like the divine right of kings were being challenged. Even the monarchy itself was ultimately questioned. On the other hand, this was also a time of intense religious persecution and superstition. The Stuart era is proof that human progress is not a strictly linear development.

Becoming a World Power

While the Stuart era had its fair share of difficulties, at the end of it, England was positioned to become the dominant world power over the course of the next century. How is that possible?

Although England had internal disagreements during the Stuart era, that did not prevent it from getting involved in what was going on in the world at large. The 17th century was a time of colonization and foreign conflict. Europe's leading powers like Spain, France, the Netherlands, and England were busily trying to expand their empires and gain more control over lucrative trade. Wars like the Anglo-Dutch Wars and the War of the Spanish Succession were part of this vie for power.

While we often think of the Elizabethan era as the grand time of exploration, England's colonial empire did not start to gain traction until the Stuart era. After all, the first American settlement of Jamestown was named after the first Stuart king, James I. It was during this era that most of the thirteen American colonies were founded, as well as settlements in Canada and the Caribbean (which proved to be the most lucrative thanks to the sugar trade). If the Elizabethan era was about exploration, the Stuart era was about colonization, and that practice proved to be far more permanently beneficial for England's economy and power.

England arrived somewhat late to the colonization game compared to other European powers. The American and Canadian settlements were largely all that was left for England since Spain had already seized most of the southern New World. However, by the ending years of the Stuart era, England (or rather Britain) had carved out an empire for itself. Successes in the War of the Spanish Succession at the beginning of the 18th century gave England access to more colonies, which helped to build its trading empire. The wealth these colonies provided then gave England the resources it needed to continue expanding and fend off its rivals.

Despite events like the English Civil War and the Glorious Revolution, England came out of the Stuart era in a very strong position globally. England's main rivals (the Netherlands, France, and Spain) were war-torn and weary. England had a firm grasp on the New World and several profitable trade routes. English power would only continue to grow over the next two centuries.

So, while the Stuart era saw major internal conflicts, England did manage to come out on top against its foreign rivals by the end of the period.

The Legacy of the Stuarts

Centuries after the end of both dynasties, it's fairly obvious that the Stuarts will never have the personal magnetism that the Tudors managed to craft. However, in terms of national success, England was not much worse off under the Stuarts than it was under the Tudors. The monarch was just gradually becoming less essential to the country's overall state.

The last Stuart monarch, Queen Anne, is a prime example of how far this separation between the monarch and the government had gotten by the end of the Stuart era. Queen Anne, although she did desire to personally rule, was often sick and unable to manage the daily running of the country. The major events of her reign, such as the War of the Spanish Succession and the union with Scotland, were largely devised and carried out by her government. She still had the ultimate say, but she was strongly influenced by those closest to her. The government under Anne was a battle between the two major parties in Parliament, the Whigs and the Tories, rather than a battle between the monarch and Parliament.

We are still a long way off from the monarch becoming a figurehead, but in the Stuart era, it was becoming clearer that the monarch could not rule alone. Parliament held the real power, and no monarch could rule without its consent. If the Tudors turned the English monarchy into a grand myth where the monarch was the embodiment of the nation itself, then the Stuarts were the reality check. The nation had grown to be bigger than its ruler.

Chapter 3: The Monarchy in Early Modern England

The early modern period of English history saw the rise and fall of two royal lines and the reigns of twelve monarchs. During this time, the monarch wielded absolute power, so these kings and queens truly steered the English nation's course. Some of them were beloved, and others were vehemently disliked. Some of them were successful, while others can only be described as failures.

For better or worse, this was the last grand age of royal power in England since the next period would see the monarch's power wane. Let's take a closer look at these twelve men and women.

Henry VII (r. 1485–1509)

Henry VII.
https://commons.wikimedia.org/wiki/File:Henry_Tudor_of_England.jpg

The early modern period began with Henry VII's victory at Bosworth and the founding of the Tudor dynasty. Henry VII's victory put an end to the bloodshed of the Wars of the Roses. To further solidify the peace, Henry VII married Elizabeth of York, the daughter of Edward IV. With this marriage, the opposing sides of Lancaster and York were united, and the chaos was finally over.

Henry's marriage shows just how aware he was of the nation's state. The Wars of the Roses had created so much chaos that it also drastically destabilized the English monarchy. When Henry VII took the throne in 1485, he needed to restrengthen the king's position, which wasn't easy. Throughout his reign, Henry VII had to deal with multiple Yorkist uprisings and plots. While Edward V and his brother Richard had been pronounced dead by their uncle Richard III, their bodies had never been found. Imposters claiming to be either Edward or Richard or even other members of the House of York popped up at the head of uprisings and were backed by Henry VII's powerful opponents.

Despite the odds, Henry managed to quell the uprisings and undermine the plots against him. Unfortunately, taking over an unstable throne and having to constantly deal with these issues made Henry VII distrustful and hard. By the time he died in 1509, his suspicious nature had made him hated or at least not well-liked.

However, Henry VII was a hard-working and efficient king who succeeded in bringing stability back to the English throne after such a long period of chaos. He passed a much different throne to his son than what he had started with in 1485.

Henry VIII (r. 1509–1547)

Henry VIII by Hans Holbein.
https://commons.wikimedia.org/wiki/File:Henry_VIII_Chatsworth.jpg

Henry VIII is one of the most famous English kings, and there's a good reason for that. His marital troubles have become the source of songs and plays, as well as being the catalyst that separated England from the Catholic Church. This part of Henry VIII's reign is so interesting that we have an entire chapter on it later, which is why we are not going to dive into that here. So, aside from marrying six different women and breaking up with the pope, what else did Henry VIII do?

In some ways, Henry VIII was the opposite of his father. While Henry VII had created policies, overseen the Crown's funds, and, in general, ran the kingdom with his own two hands, Henry VIII relied more on his councilors. Men like Thomas Wolsey, Thomas More, Thomas Cranmer, and Thomas Cromwell (Thomas was a very popular name with Henry VIII) were the ones running the show. That might make Henry VIII sound like a pushover, but that is far from the truth. Henry VIII had no problem interfering with the business that he mostly left to his councilors. These men only lasted as long as they did what Henry VIII wanted, and for all of them, like Henry VIII's wives, there came a time when the king no longer had a use for them. Henry VIII's reliance on his councilors, therefore, had more to do with the fact that he would rather be doing something else.

It could also be argued that Henry VIII's less hands-on style of kingship was better for the nation because when he did decide to take things into his own hands, they didn't go very well. He involved England in costly foreign wars and worsened its relationship with Scotland. His reign also saw the rise of growing religious tensions, but the fault for that cannot be laid entirely at the king's door. This was the era of the Reformation. Growing religious tensions were everywhere in Europe at this time.

In terms of pure ruling effectiveness, Henry VII was likely a better king than his son, but Henry VIII was more well-liked. He was a vibrant and young man when he took the throne, and he breathed life back into Henry VII's suspicious court. While Henry VIII may not have understood how to make effective policies, he did understand how to look like a king. He brought a charm and grandeur that has made him a lasting symbol of the monarchy.

Edward VI (r. 1547–1553)

Edward VI by William Scrots.
https://commons.wikimedia.org/wiki/File:Edward_VI_of_England_c._1546.jpg

Although Henry VIII was married six times, when he died in 1547, he had only one male heir, the child of his third wife, Jane Seymour. Nine-year-old Edward became king after his father's death, and he died only six years later at the age of fifteen. History remembers Edward VI as the "Boy King."

Since Edward VI came to the throne at such a young age, he was simply a symbol through, with other men ruling through him. The first man was Edward Seymour, the Duke of Somerset and the king's uncle. Somerset was overthrown and replaced by John Dudley, the Duke of Northumberland. Both Seymour and Dudley took steps while in control to confirm the Reformation, which was in keeping with Edward VI's own religious zeal and strong devotion to Protestantism.

Edward VI's early death naturally meant there were no direct heirs. Edward VI planned to pass the throne not to one of his half-sisters (Mary and Elizabeth) but to Lady Jane Grey, who was John Dudley's daughter-in-law. This was not carried out after Edward

VI's death. Jane Grey lasted all of nine days before she was replaced by Henry VIII's eldest daughter Mary.

Mary I (r. 1553–1558) and Philip (r. 1554–1558)

Queen Mary Tudor by Antonis Mor.
https://commons.wikimedia.org/wiki/File:Maria_Tudor1.jpg

Mary I was the first woman to ever rule England in her own right, but she is not remembered fondly, largely because of one fatal flaw. She was Roman Catholic.

Mary I was the daughter of Henry VIII and Catherine of Aragon. Soon after ascending to the throne in 1553, she married Spanish Prince Philip (who soon became the Spanish king, Philip II), despite the warnings of her advisers. This marriage to a Catholic was part of Mary I's attempts to bring her nation back into the Roman Church. However, by this time, the "damage" of the Reformation had impacted England. The country did not look kindly on her marriage to Philip, but Mary I had her father's stubborn streak. Despite a Protestant revolt, she married Philip anyway, who, as part of the conditions for their marriage, became co-monarch rather than simply her husband.

After her marriage, Mary I tried her hardest to turn England back to Catholicism. She persecuted the Protestants, whom she saw as heretics, burning around three hundred people at the stake. This campaign had the opposite effect of what Mary had hoped for. It earned her the nickname Bloody Mary and caused the people to hate her. It is unclear just how deep the resentment toward Mary I went during her lifetime. Since England stayed Protestant, Mary I has been viewed as a villain, but we must also remember that England's break with Rome had happened only twenty years prior to her reign. There were probably many Catholics remaining in England while Mary I was alive. However, as time passed and England became more Protestant, Mary I's posthumous reputation only deteriorated.

Elizabeth I (r. 1558–1603)

Elizabeth I, "The Pelican Portrait," by Nicholas Hilliard.
https://commons.wikimedia.org/wiki/File:Nicholas_Hilliard_Elizabeth_I_The_Pelican_Portrait.jpg

Henry VIII had only one remaining child. Elizabeth I was the last of the Tudors and arguably the best of them. Even now, she remains one of England's most well-remembered and beloved rulers, and she is the only monarch of the early modern period to have an era named after her (the Elizabethan Age). So, what made Elizabeth I such a good leader?

Elizabeth I had an interesting and, at times, incredibly dangerous upbringing before her ascension to the throne. At the age of three, her mother was beheaded, and she was declared illegitimate. She had to survive through the reigns of both her half-siblings, where she was seen as a potentially volatile spark for any rebellions or discontent, especially under the reign of Mary I. To survive in these circumstances, Elizabeth I learned from an early age an enormous amount of self-control. She was able to show people exactly what they wanted to see, carefully controlling her actions and reputation to best suit her needs.

This quality continued to serve Elizabeth I well once she took the throne. She was an expert at putting on a show and crafting herself into a symbol of both the monarchy and the nation itself. Instead of allowing her sex to be used against her (there was pervading sexism at this time), she painted herself as the mother of the nation, creating a sense of love and devotion. This strict attention to how she presented herself also meant that she was fairly unreadable. Elizabeth I could be generous when it benefited her and wrathful when pushed. There was a sense that no one knew what Queen Elizabeth thought, and she used that air of mystery to play rival factions against each other in her court, maintaining firm if not absolute control of her government.

To put it simply, Elizabeth I was one of England's most politically savvy monarchs. She could work both a crowd and individuals to her advantage. There can be no doubt that England prospered under her rule. To this day, the Elizabethan Age is viewed as a golden era of English history.

James I (r. 1603–1625)

James I by John De Critz.
https://commons.wikimedia.org/wiki/File:James_VI_and_I.jpg

We discussed how the throne went from the Tudors to the Stuarts in Chapter 2, so here we will focus more on James I as a monarch.

When James I became king of England, he had already ruled Scotland for around thirty-seven years. It was true that he was only one year old when he took the throne, but nevertheless, thirty-seven years was a long time. This gave him an advantage few other monarchs had when they ascended the throne: experience. In many ways, James I's experience as king of Scotland served him well in England. His policies were often reasonable and effective, but there were ways in which James I's experience hurt him in England.

Having already been a king for so long, James I had a very clear idea of what kingship ought to be. He believed in the absolute authority of the king, which brought him into conflict with a uniquely English institution: Parliament. Parliament had been around in England since the 13th century and had grown in authority and its willingness to question the English monarch. It was Parliament that held the right to levy taxes, which made raising funds for the government practically impossible without Parliament's approval.

James I had dealt with assemblies in Scotland, but he had no idea how to deal with the English Parliament. James I came into frequent conflict with Parliament, and in 1611, he dissolved it. Parliament would not meet again for ten years (except for a brief meeting in 1614). During this time, James I had to find other ways to raise money since he could not create taxes without Parliament. These other means, such as the sale of monopolies, were often unpopular and did not improve the king's image. James I's lack of respect for the Parliament did not have drastic consequences in his lifetime, but it did set the stage for the civil war that would break out during his son's reign.

However, what James I is most famous for is something that had little effect on his reign: the King James Bible. James I authorized this translation of the Bible in 1604 and approved the list of scholars assigned to the project. The translation was completed and published in 1611 and remains one of the most popular English translations of the Bible to this day. The King James Bible has proved to be the most lasting legacy of the first Stuart monarch.

Charles I (r. 1625–1649)

Charles I by Anthony van Dyck.
https://commons.wikimedia.org/wiki/File:Van_Dyck,_Sir_Anthony_-_Charles_I_-_Google_Art_Project.jpg

The monarchs of early modern England have their share of successes and failures, but Charles I might just be the biggest failure of them all. Charles I's reign saw the outbreak of a civil war, which ended with his execution and resulted in an eleven-year span during which England had no king or queen.

We will cover the details of the English Civil War in Chapter 10, but for now, let's talk about what the problem was with Charles I. What was so bad about this king that caused England to decide they didn't want any king?

Like his father, James I, Charles I was a proponent of royal absolutism and the divine right of kings, which meant that kings get their right to rule from God and thus are subject to no earthly authority. The Catholic Church could have still presented a check to the king's power, but during the Stuart era, England was no longer Catholic. The king was the head of the church and the government, and based on the divine right of kings, this gave him absolute and supreme power.

You can begin to see just what kind of king this doctrine made. Charles I did not believe that anyone had the right to question or challenge him. He refused to listen to Parliament and the complaints of his kingdom's magnates. This eventually led to a civil war, but it caused an even greater problem when the war was over.

Although Charles I had been defeated, he refused to negotiate with the victors. He would make no concessions. He wouldn't even talk to his captors. Finding the king so intractable, Parliament eventually convicted him of treason. Charles I was beheaded on January 30th, 1649.

Not only did Charles I's reign get him beheaded, but it also caused England to abandon the monarchy for a while. After Charles I's death, England entered an eleven-year period known as the Interregnum (between kings). After these eleven years, England decided the problem may not have been monarchs in general but Charles I specifically. They decided to restore the monarchy and invited Charles I's son to return and take the throne.

Charles II (r. 1660–1685)

Charles II by John Michael Wright.
(Public domain: https://commons.wikimedia.org/wiki/File:John_Michael_Wright_(1617-94)_-_Charles_II_(1630-1685)_-_RCIN_404951_-_Royal_Collection_-_1.jpg)

Charles II's ascension to the English throne could have been a very messy affair. After all, Charles II was returning from the continent after having to flee England in fear of his life. Even though the people of England had decided they wanted a king again, there was much anxiety in inviting Charles II to take the throne. Wouldn't he want to seek revenge against those who had murdered his father? The members of Parliament were understandably worried.

As messy as it might have been, the restoration of the monarchy went surprisingly smoothly, thanks in large part to the council of Edward Hyde, the Earl of Clarendon. Under Hyde's guidance, Charles II issued a general pardon for crimes committed during the English Civil War and the Interregnum. This meant that Charles II wouldn't be taking revenge on his father's enemies. The leaders of England were so relieved to hear they wouldn't be losing their heads that they welcomed Charles II back with open arms.

As a ruler, Charles II was neither the worst nor the best English monarch. He was known as a man who enjoyed his pleasures, and he was very good at letting his advisers take the fall for his bad policies. During his reign, he faced a lot of religious discontentment. Charles II's attempts to allow more religious tolerance were firmly shut down by Parliament, and fear of the throne passing to his Catholic brother, James, was rampant in the late years of his rule.

However, Charles II managed to delicately balance these tensions and kept the peace until he died in 1685. He was a king with enough political skills to secure his own position, but he lacked the inspiration necessary to truly solve the problem. When he died without a legitimate heir, his brother James was left facing the issues that Charles II had only delayed.

James II (r. 1685–1688)

James II by Godfrey Kneller.
https://commons.wikimedia.org/wiki/File:King_James_II.jpg

If the Stuarts' luck had appeared to be improving with the restoration of Charles II, it took a downward turn with his brother, James II. James II only ruled for three years before his reign ended in the Glorious Revolution and the installment of Mary II and William III. James II was the only English monarch in the entire early modern period to be forced to leave the throne while he was still alive. What was so bad about James II? The answer is similar to the problem with Mary I. James II was Roman Catholic.

Thanks to the Reformation, religious tensions in Europe were at an all-time high. In England, the fear and hatred of Roman Catholics had reached levels of almost paranoia. We will discuss more of why exactly this was in later chapters, but suffice it to say, it was not good for James II, who was a member of the Catholic

Church.

To be fair to James II, from an objective viewpoint, it doesn't seem like his religion affected his ability to rule an Anglican nation all that much. James II was a capable military commander who served his brother Charles II well, and his daughters, Mary and Anne, were raised Protestant. Unlike Mary I, it didn't seem like James II was planning to bring the English nation back under Rome's guiding hand, but by the time of his reign, the mistrust of Catholics was much greater than it had been when Mary I held the throne.

So, when James II took the throne in 1685, the nation simply did not trust him. He had to deal with two rebellions almost immediately, which soured the new king's opinion of his subjects. James II became mistrustful and began favoring Roman Catholics, seeking to overturn the laws against them. Unfortunately, in 17th-century England, religious tolerance was not a popular move. Three short years after James II's reign had begun, he found himself facing a usurper, William of Orange, who had been invited there by his own people. When James II's largely Protestant army refused to stand with him, he was forced to abdicate and flee the country. His Protestant daughter Mary, along with her husband William, took the throne with relatively little bloodshed, which earned this event the name of the Glorious Revolution.

Mary II (r. 1689–1694) and William III (r. 1689–1702)

Mary II by Peter Lely.
https://commons.wikimedia.org/wiki/File:1662_Mary_II.jpg

William III technically seized the English throne through force when his arrival with an army forced James II to abdicate. However, he also invaded at the request of English leaders, so William III has the strange claim of being a welcomed conquering king.

Because William outlived his wife by eight years, history tends to remember William of Orange or William III more than his wife, Mary II. However, it was through Mary that William had a claim to the English throne. Mary II was the daughter of James II and the next in line after her father abdicated. She was offered the throne, and she insisted that her husband reign as co-monarch. While Mary II was still alive, she technically shared power with William III, but she simply followed his lead and direction in almost everything, making William III the ruler.

As king of England, William III was extremely interested in foreign affairs and spent a good deal of his reign campaigning in Europe. He was particularly concerned about preventing the French from expanding their control but was often frustrated by the English Parliament's lack of enthusiasm for his cause. Time proved William III right, as England would join the War of the Spanish Succession against the French shortly after William III's death.

The matter of the war with France summarizes William III's reign. He was a relatively effective king who was still disliked by the English court for being a foreigner. Still, he was well-liked by the general people because of his Protestantism, and his time as the king saw the English Crown stabilize.

Anne (r. 1702–1714)

Queen Anne by Edmond Lilly.
https://commons.wikimedia.org/wiki/File:Queen_Anne_Lilly.jpg

The final Stuart monarch and the final monarch in the early modern period was the second daughter of James II, Anne. Although their father was ferociously disliked by the English people, both Mary and Anne escaped his legacy because they did not share their father's fatal flaw. They were not Catholic; they were Protestant.

As queen, Anne never gained the independence that she wanted. She was often ill, leaving the government largely in the hands of her advisers. The major policies of this government were centered around the war that her predecessor, William III, had predicted, the War of the Spanish Succession, which lasted the entirety of Anne's twelve-year reign.

Although Anne was pregnant many times, she had no surviving children, which meant her death was viewed with some anxiety. English leaders were afraid that James the Old Pretender, the son of James II, would make a move for the throne. To prevent the English throne from passing into Catholic hands, the Hanovers, who were descended from James I, were selected to succeed the Stuart dynasty.

The Stuart dynasty ended very similarly to the Tudors, with the death of a childless queen, and like with the passing of the throne from the Tudors to the Stuarts, the transition from the Stuarts to the Hanovers was surprisingly smooth. Despite low points with Charles I and James II, the English monarchy in the early modern period was a relatively stable institution at the height of its power. English monarchs would soon never again wield the power they did in this age. By the end of the 18th century, the monarch would be little more than a figurehead.

Chapter 4: Key English Figures from 1485 to 1714

When talking about important people in the early modern era, it's easy to get caught up with the royalty. After all, royalty in this period did wield real power, and so every English king and queen, whether they were good or bad, had an enormous impact on the nation.

However, that does not mean that England did not produce other figures that steered the course of history and whose impact we continue to feel today. Some of the key English figures from this period have had a far wider and longer-lasting impact than the monarchs. The following figures are listed in chronological order based on their births.

Mary, Queen of Scots

There are quite a few famous Marys from this period, but for pure drama, Mary, Queen of Scots has to be the most interesting. Born in 1542, Mary was the only child of James V of Scotland. When her father died six days after her birth, she became queen of Scotland.

No one actually expects a six-day-old to rule, so Mary's mother became regent. Mary was sent off to France, where she was raised in Henry II's court. Although Mary received a thorough education in France, her French upbringing would ultimately prove to be far more harmful than helpful. She was pampered and raised as a

Roman Catholic, and at the age of eighteen, when she returned to rule Scotland in her own right, she found herself at the head of a tempestuous Protestant nation.

Mary was not well equipped for the role in which she found herself, but she still might have made a tolerable queen had she made wiser decisions in love. Her marriage to Lord Darnley was a love match, but it proved disastrous. Darnley was not well-liked, and by marrying him, Mary managed to agitate many of the Scottish nobles, including her half-brother, who had been of great help to Mary up until that point.

Mary soon realized her mistake. A year after their marriage, Darnley murdered Mary's secretary in front of her, and Mary began to realize just what sort of man she had married. It is unclear if Mary played a part in what happened next, but the intolerable Darnley soon met his end. In 1567, the house where Darnley was staying blew up, killing him.

This might have been a chance for Mary to turn things around, but after three short months, she married again. And she again chose poorly. This husband, Lord Bothwell, was the chief suspect in the murder of Mary's previous husband, and he was not any more liked by the Scottish nobility than Darnley had been. Before the end of the year, Bothwell had been exiled, and Mary was forced to step down. The crown of Scotland passed to her one-year-old son, James.

Like a real-life soap opera, losing the throne of Scotland was not the end of Mary's troubles. After all of this, Mary fled to England, seeking sanctuary with her cousin, Queen Elizabeth. That was a mistake. As Elizabeth's cousin, Mary was the next in line to the throne of England and, thus, in Elizabeth's eyes, her rival. After Mary arrived in England, Queen Elizabeth kept her imprisoned for the next eighteen years.

Unfortunately, Mary's tale was not meant to end happily. As a Roman Catholic and the next in line to the English throne, Mary was the natural core around which English Catholics gathered. They wished to return England to Catholicism. When a conspiracy was discovered in 1586 to assassinate Queen Elizabeth and replace her with the Catholic Mary, Elizabeth I had had enough. She decided that her cousin was too big of a threat. Mary, Queen of Scots was executed in 1587.

To this day, historians argue about how much Mary was to blame for the woes that befell her. She has been seen as both a tragic figure and a scheming murderer. Whatever she was, her life is certainly proof that fact can be just as dramatic as fiction.

William Shakespeare

William Shakespeare.
Rodrio22, CC BY-SA 4.0 <https://creativecommons.org/licenses/by-sa/4.0>, via Wikimedia Commons: https://commons.wikimedia.org/wiki/File:William_Shakespeare_2022.jpg

If there is a competition for the most well-remembered and idolized figure from early modern England, then William Shakespeare is the undisputed winner. He was born around 1564 and died in 1616. During his lifetime, Shakespeare wrote 38 plays and over 150 poems. In the four hundred years since his death, he has come to be widely regarded as one of the best, if not the best, English writers of all time. The Bard is so praised and widespread that you practically cannot get a high school education in English without reading Shakespeare.

Because he is so adored by scholars and teachers, many people today associate Shakespeare with elitism and pretentiousness. However, to be fair to the Bard, it pays to put him in the context of his own time. When he was alive, Shakespeare was less of what we would today call an artist and more of an entertainer. Standing room in one of the period's outdoor theaters was cheap enough that pretty much anyone could afford it, and live theater, in general, was seen as entertainment for the unwashed masses.

Live theater was so far from being considered a high-end pursuit that many people believed it to be a terrible influence. Theaters were not allowed in the city of London itself, so they were instead built on the other side of the Thames River in Southwark, an area that was home to other institutions not wanted in the city proper, such as brothels and bear-baiting arenas. The Globe Theatre was even located next to a bear-baiting arena, and the theater used the blood from the arena for performances.

So, Shakespeare is not as fancy as you might think. His language may feel incredibly sophisticated today, but that has more to do with the fact that it was written four hundred years ago and less to do with Shakespeare trying to be pretentious. If you take the time to dissect some of Shakespeare's plays, you'll find them full of bawdy jokes and witty lines.

Does this mean that Shakespeare isn't as great as people make him out to be? If anything, it should make him better. Shakespeare was so good with words that even though he was writing for entertainment and didn't even make up most of his own stories, he is still the gold standard in English literature four hundred years later.

Guy Fawkes

If you're not from the United Kingdom, you probably see nothing special about the 5th of November, but in the UK, it's Guy Fawkes Day. You might be thinking that Guy Fawkes must have done something pretty great to earn an entire holiday, but that's not the reason this figure from early modern England has his own holiday.

Guy Fawkes is famous for being one of the conspirators behind the Gunpowder Plot, which was an attempt by Roman Catholics to blow up Parliament on November 5th, 1605. The conspirators hoped that by killing the king and other English leaders, there would be enough confusion for Catholics to seize control of the country. When the plot was discovered, it had the opposite effect of what the plotters had intended. News of a Catholic plot to kill the king only increased the fear and hatred of Catholics in England, and even stricter laws were enacted to restrict Catholics as a result.

Ironically, Guy Fawkes was not the leader of the plot. The conspiracy was headed by Robert Catesby. However, Fawkes was the one caught guarding the barrels of gunpowder and was arrested, tortured, and executed.

That wasn't enough, though. November 5th became a national holiday, and effigies of Guy Fawkes are still burned on this day. Guy Fawkes was not the leader of the conspirators, nor did he succeed in killing the king, but he remains perhaps the most infamous person from early modern England.

Oliver Cromwell

Although his name might not be as familiar as Shakespeare or Guy Fawkes, Oliver Cromwell is easily one of the most influential figures in English history. When England found itself without a monarch during the Interregnum, Oliver Cromwell ruled the nation as Lord Protector.

Who was Cromwell, and how did he land such a high position? Kings and queens are afforded the right to rule by virtue of their birth, but what virtue placed Oliver Cromwell at the head of England from 1653 to 1658?

Born in 1599, Oliver Cromwell lived a fairly uneventful life for his first thirty years. Just before he turned thirty, though, Cromwell converted to Christianity, which would have a profound impact on him. With the awakening of his religious zeal, Cromwell became far more active in politics. He was a Puritan and spoke out against the authority of the bishops, believing that congregations should be able to pick their own ministers instead of having them appointed by the king. Because of his religious views, Cromwell began to oppose Charles I's government.

If Cromwell had been nothing more than a deeply religious man, history likely would not have remembered him, but when the English Civil War broke out, Cromwell proved himself to be a soldier as well. As Parliament faced the king in open warfare, Oliver

Cromwell rose through the ranks as a practical and effective leader. Cromwell's success as a soldier made him the head of the army, making him the most powerful man in England after the death of Charles I.

Still, Cromwell did not exactly leap into Charles I's place. It took four years after the king's execution before Cromwell became Lord Protector. For those four years, Parliament attempted to govern, but there was much distrust between Parliament and the army, which made an effective government difficult. Cromwell himself disliked the radical republicanism promoted by some members of Parliament, believing that a more moderate course was necessary to reestablish stability and prosperity in England. He eventually accepted the position as Lord Protector, conceding that providence (God) seemed to will that it be so.

That might sound like a thin cover-up of his ambitions, but whether you agree with him or not, it does appear that Cromwell took his religion seriously. He believed that he was following God's wishes in becoming the most powerful man in England.

Despite having been one of the men to sign the king's death warrant, Cromwell was rather conservative as Lord Protector. He did want reform, especially in increasing religious tolerance, but he butted heads with the more radical members of Parliament, who were far more interested in redoing the constitution. Cromwell feared that dissolving England's traditional government would only result in anarchy. His desire to maintain stability resulted in a government that resembled a constitutional monarchy rather than a republic. This resemblance to a monarchy was confirmed when Cromwell named his son Richard as his successor shortly before his death in 1658.

To this day, people's opinion of Oliver Cromwell is divided. He has been seen as a dictator who used his military power to seize control of the nation. He has been viewed as a religious fanatic who used his belief in divine providence to justify his actions. He has also been criticized for halting the radical reinvention of the English government, and he has been praised for restoring and maintaining order in England with his more moderate reform approach. Whatever your opinion of him, it is clear that Oliver Cromwell was a highly capable man. For good or ill, he seized and maintained effective control of the English government for five years, making him the only self-made English ruler from this period.

Edward Hyde (Earl of Clarendon)

Edward Hyde by Peter Lely.
https://commons.wikimedia.org/wiki/File:Peter_Lely_(1618-1680)_(after)_-_Sir_Edward_Hyde_(1609%E2%80%931674),_1st_Earl_of_Clarendon_-_1257076_-_National_Trust.jpg

Speaking of English rulers, you likely got the impression from the last chapter that some monarchs were better than others. Since the monarchs had control over the government, what happened when the king or queen was lazy or incompetent? Who ran the country when the monarch didn't feel like it?

Although history tends not to remember their names nearly as well, most of England's monarchs had close advisers. These people often helped steer the course of England as much as the monarch. People like Robert Cecil under Queen Elizabeth I, Sarah Churchill under Queen Anne, John Dudley under Edward VI, and Thomas Wolsey and Thomas Cromwell under Henry VIII all wielded enormous influence because the monarch turned to them for advice and, in many cases, gave them powerful positions.

There were so many people that stood behind the monarchs of this period that we can't possibly begin to discuss them all, but as an example, we will look at one man who stood behind two kings and greatly impacted English history—Edward Hyde.

Edward Hyde is more commonly known by his title as the Earl of Clarendon or simply Clarendon. He was born in 1609 and served as an adviser to both Charles I and Charles II. Under Charles I, Hyde attempted to advise the king to take a more moderate approach in his conflict with Parliament but to little avail. The situation erupted into the English Civil War, and Hyde was sent to the continent as the young prince's guardian.

Hyde's service to Charles II proved just how capable he truly was. The Declaration of Breda of 1660 was Hyde's handiwork and allowed for Charles II's peaceful restoration to his father's throne. Once restored to his throne, Charles II relied heavily on Hyde, who became the first earl of Clarendon a year later in 1661. Clarendon (Hyde) was a competent administrator, but he eventually learned, like many close royal advisers, the dangers of being so close to the Crown.

In a monarchy, the king can do no wrong. You cannot impeach a king, so the king's close advisers are often forced to take the fall for government failures. By 1667, Clarendon's age (he was fifty-eight) and strict sense of morality did not sit well with the court of a man known as the Merry Monarch. In the aftermath of the Second Anglo-Dutch War, which was a disaster for the English, Clarendon was made a scapegoat. Charles II allowed the blame to lay on his oldest adviser rather than on himself, and Clarendon had to flee, living the rest of his days in exile in France.

Clarendon is an example of what many royal advisers and key political figures in this period were unable to overcome—the changing whims of the monarch. Political careers rose and fell based on who the monarch favored, and even those who proved themselves capable were not protected from fickle human nature. Politics and government at this time were deeply personal, and it showed in how quickly many rose and then fell from power.

John Churchill (Duke of Marlborough)

John Churchill (left) with General Armstrong (right).
https://commons.wikimedia.org/wiki/File:Major_General_John_Armstrong_with_John_C
hurchill_1st_Duke_of_Marlborough.jpg

Known as England's greatest soldier, John Churchill is a figure from the later part of the early modern era. His military prowess was key in cementing England's position as a world power.

John Churchill was born in 1650. He began his military career at the age of seventeen and advanced steadily. By 1685, with the ascension of James II to the throne, John Churchill was the practical commander of the English military. It was at this point in his career that Churchill showed his capabilities extended to the political sphere as well. With William of Orange's invasion in 1688, Churchill saw the writing on the wall and switched sides. He abandoned the Roman Catholic James II and gave his allegiance to William. As the leader of England's army, Churchill's decision meant that James II had no army with which to oppose William.

The result was a relatively bloodless transfer of power that has come to be known as the Glorious Revolution.

Even though John Churchill's decision to side with William of Orange was a major factor in what allowed William to take the throne from James II, Churchill's career did not advance as one might expect. William was distrustful of a man who would abandon his sovereign and suspected Churchill of plotting to restore James II. Churchill's military career was thus cut short for a few years until William III needed him for a more pressing issue—stopping Louis XIV.

In 1701, it became clear that King Louis XIV of France had set his sights on the Spanish throne, and William III was determined to halt his ambitions. In such a conflict, a military mind like John Churchill was essential. Although William III would end up dying in 1702, his successor, Queen Anne, confirmed Churchill's appointment to command the forces opposing Louis XIV's bid on Spain.

It was during the War of the Spanish Succession (1701-1714) that Churchill's reputation as a soldier was truly established. He won impressive victories at Blenheim (1704), Ramillies (1706), and Oudenaarde (1708). It appeared that Churchill simply could not be beaten in battle, yet the war dragged on. Unfortunately, wars are expensive even when you are winning them. Despite Churchill's victories, support for the war in England eventually wavered, and support for Churchill went too. In 1711, Churchill was dismissed from his military command. He died eleven years later in 1722.

That was life for many key political figures of this era. There were many who shone brilliantly for a moment, but very few managed to die with their star undiminished. The early modern era was a turbulent and changing time, not just for England but also for the world. Many were able to achieve greatness, but precious few were able to maintain it.

Chapter 5: The Renaissance

The Renaissance. The word brings to mind images of marble statues, finely detailed oil paintings, and ornate clothing. It makes us think of poetry, music, and philosophy. The Renaissance is the era that started the modern age. It brought Western civilization out of the Dark Ages and ushered in a new era of enlightenment and reason.

Or did it?

We think of the Renaissance as being an era that rescued humanity from ignorance, resurrecting our interest in science and the arts. But just how true is this? And what impact did it have specifically on England?

What Was the Renaissance?

When you hear the phrase Renaissance, you likely think of art. Paintings like Leonardo da Vinci's *Mona Lisa*, sculptures like Michelangelo's *David*, and large frescoes like Raphael's *The School of Athens* are visual embodiments of the Renaissance. However, to confine the Renaissance to an artistic movement is to greatly misunderstand what it was. The Renaissance was far more than a particular artistic style.

Perhaps the easiest way to approach what the Renaissance was is to consider what the word itself means. Renaissance is French for rebirth. The Renaissance was given this name because it saw a revival of interest in the classical period (Greek and Roman civilization). The Middle Ages had largely been characterized by the domination of the Roman Catholic Church and theological thinkers, but thanks to events like the Black Death, the increasingly obvious corruption of the church, and a growing sense of nationalism, the systems of the Middle Ages were destabilizing. As their world began to transform irrevocably, people turned to other places to make sense of what was happening, which eventually led to a renewed interest in classical culture, sparking the Renaissance.

For a long time, this understanding of the Renaissance was taken to a more extreme level. The Middle Ages was seen as a dark time of ignorance, where religious dogma prevented any real sense of philosophical, artistic, or scientific progress. The reality is far more complex. Humanity did not completely stagnate during the medieval period. We now know that the Middle Ages was far richer in culture and thought than the Renaissance era would have us believe.

The phrase Middle Ages (which implies this period was somehow a pause between classical times and the Renaissance) was not used until the Renaissance. What all this means is that when Renaissance thinkers act as though they were saving humanity from a dark age, we need to take it with a grain of salt. The Renaissance was a crucial moment in European history, but it was not an absolute paradigm shift that saved Western civilization from decay.

Still, the Renaissance was a reaction to the gradual breakdown of medieval society and a time of great transformation. The movement that characterized the direction of this transformation was humanism.

Humanism, as the name implies, takes humanity as its subject. Instead of the heavy focus on God and theology that had been the drive of intellectual projects in the Middle Ages, humanists began to take a keener interest in things related to humans. That included areas of study like philosophy, history, art, drama, and more. They are the subjects that we today call the humanities because they involve the study of humans at some level.

This interest in humanity affected not only what people were thinking and studying but also led to deeper shifts in the culture. The medieval period's interest in God had placed humanity in a less than dignified position. There was a great emphasis on the value of penance in the Middle Ages. Humanism, in contrast, asserted the dignity of man. Life was not about penance but about striving to achieve creative greatness. It was this belief that provided the push for the scientific, philosophical, and artistic achievements of the Renaissance.

Knowing all that, how do we answer the question of what was the Renaissance? The Renaissance was a shift in intellectual focus from God to humanity in response to the failures of medieval society. It saw a greatly renewed interest in classical culture and thought and resulted in many achievements in the areas of art and science.

Where Did It Start and How Did It Spread?

Now that we have a better idea of what the Renaissance was, let's turn to the matter of geography and timing. Much like a disease, intellectual movements like the Renaissance often have a point of origin and a method through which they are transmitted.

The time is the late 13th century, and the place is Italy. The Renaissance itself had not yet gotten underway, but it is here that we find the seeds that would sprout into the Renaissance. By this time, the problems with medieval society were becoming more and more apparent. By the early 14th century, men like Dante (the author of the *Divine Comedy*), Giotto (an artist), and Petrarch (a poet and scholar) were showing humanist interests and styles in their work. This was the proto-Renaissance, and it seemed like a fully-fledged Renaissance would soon develop. However, thanks to the outbreak of plague known as the Black Death and several internal conflicts, the 14th century proved to be a rough time for Italians, and the movement that we can see beginning with Dante, Giotto, and Petrarch nearly disappeared.

In the 15th century, a level of stability returned, and the Renaissance truly emerged in Italy. In cities like Florence, the arts flourished, and when these artists studied and imitated classical styles, they revived interest in Greco-Roman culture. The

Renaissance had arrived.

The Renaissance clearly got its start in Italy, but how did it spread throughout Europe and all the way to England? In the present day, we often take for granted our ability to find information quickly. Thanks to the internet, the world is more connected than ever, but back in the medieval and early modern era, this was clearly not the case. New ideas took time to spread. Had it not been for one very important invention, the Renaissance would likely not have had the impact it did outside of Italy. That invention was the printing press.

The earliest printing press to appear in Europe was Johannes Gutenberg's. Gutenberg's press appeared around the middle of the 15th century and could print around 250 sheets per hour. While that may not sound impressive today, before the invention of the mechanized printing press, the only way to copy books was by hand, which meant there were no mass-produced books. Without the ability to produce many copies of a book, there was no way to spread and share information.

The importance of the printing press in both the Renaissance and later in the Reformation cannot be overstated. With the ability to mass-produce books, both education and religion were forever changed. Students could now study classical writers, and everyone (and by everyone, we mean everyone who could read, which was still a small portion of the population) could read the Bible. This access to knowledge, in large part, made the Renaissance possible. Without the printing press, the renewed interest in classical thought and culture would never have been able to reach as many people as it did.

Gutenberg era printing press.
https://commons.wikimedia.org/wiki/File:Gutenberg.press.jpg

The printing press was not the only reason the Renaissance took off the way it did, though. In 1492, Christopher Columbus landed in the Bahamas, discovering two entire continents of which Europeans had no knowledge. In later chapters, we will discuss this exploration in more detail, but in terms of understanding the Renaissance, this Age of Exploration was a vital contributing factor. Europeans at this time were contending with the fact that the world was much larger than they had realized. This new awareness brought greater levels of scientific inquiry and simple curiosity that helped to drive the desire for knowledge that characterized much of the Renaissance at a fundamental level.

That's a basic overview of how the Renaissance started and spread, but how did it end? In one sense, the Renaissance didn't end, as the ideas that it sparked continued to develop and create the modern world. However, in terms of the artistic style and intense interest in classical culture, the Renaissance did end, and the event that is typically used to mark that end is the Sack of Rome by the Holy Roman Empire's forces in 1527.

The Sack of Rome is used to mark the end of the Renaissance largely because it disrupted and ended the Renaissance in its place of origin, Italy. However, looking at the Renaissance on a more

European-wide scale, the end was far more gradual. Ultimately, the Reformation brought an end to much of the Renaissance. The Renaissance era's reverence for classical culture created much tension with the Christian faith. As religious issues exploded with the Reformation, this tension became more and more unbearable, eventually causing the decline of humanism, which had defined the Renaissance era.

What Did the Renaissance Look Like?

We have mentioned several times that the Renaissance saw great achievements in art, but what exactly does that include? What made Renaissance art so different?

The Renaissance produced many talented artists, but there are three who stand out as the quintessential Renaissance man: Leonardo da Vinci, Michelangelo, and Raphael. By taking a glance at these three men, we can better understand both the art of the Renaissance and the Renaissance itself.

Leonardo da Vinci was truly a Renaissance man in that his interests and skills covered a wide array of subjects. The Renaissance was not an era of specialization but a time when all knowledge and truth were believed to be intimately connected. You may know Leonardo da Vinci as the artist who painted the *Mona Lisa*, but did you know he was also an engineer, an architect, and a scientist who studied things ranging from anatomy to flight? Leonardo was a busy man, and what he captures about the period is an underlying desire for knowledge. The Renaissance was about far more than painting. Humanism sought greater knowledge of humanity, and that desire for knowledge found expression in many ways.

Mona Lisa by Leonardo da Vinci.
https://commons.wikimedia.org/wiki/File:Mona_Lisa,_by_Leonardo_da_Vinci,_from_C2 RMF_retouched.jpg)

If the Renaissance was about the knowledge of humanity, why was art such a key part of it? Those two ideas may seem disconnected, but in this period, art was highly valued as a type of knowledge. Our understanding of the world comes largely through our sight, and the visual arts were, therefore, a means to record these observations. At the time, art was almost mathematical in nature. For instance, Raphael's work shows a great adherence to balance and harmony. Art allowed man to order what he saw of the world, and in doing so, it was believed that man could come to understand himself and his place in the world better.

The School of Athens by Raphael.
https://commons.wikimedia.org/wiki/File:%22The_School_of_Athens%22_by_Raffaello_Sanzio_da_Urbino.jpg

Michelangelo's work, in particular, displays an interest in understanding humanity. Michelangelo considered himself a sculptor before all else, and his sculptures, such as the *David* and the *Pieta*, show admiration for the human form. His paintings, such as his work on the Sistine Chapel, display the human form boldly. This is what made art so important in the Renaissance. Artists like Michelangelo argued for the dignity of man in the way in which they visually represented people. Their art declares the beauty of the human form in a way that art in the Middle Ages had never done.

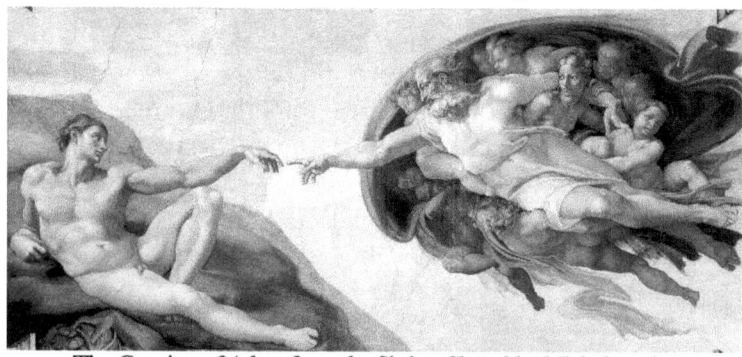

The Creation of Adam from the Sistine Chapel by Michelangelo.
https://commons.wikimedia.org/wiki/File:Creation_of_Adam,_Michelangelo_(1475%E2%80%931564),_circa_1511.jpg

In Italy, the Renaissance clearly found expression in the visual arts, but in other places, other aspects of culture flourished. The Renaissance in England looked quite different from its Italian muse.

The Renaissance and England

Despite the greatly increased printing speed of Gutenberg's printing press, the people were nowhere near the speed at which information spreads around the globe today. Intellectual movements moved slower than the plague in the early modern era. It was not until the 16th century that the Renaissance reached the shores of England.

The Wars of the Roses had ended the medieval period in England and left the country in shambles. While the Renaissance was taking off in the late 15th century in Italy, in England, the first Tudor king, Henry VII, was performing the monumental task of restoring order and stability. It was not until Henry VII's son, Henry VIII, took the throne that England could focus on culture.

In several ways, Henry VIII was a Renaissance king. He could write poetry and play music. He was aware of and interested in the humanist movement, and his court included many great humanist thinkers, such as Thomas More. However, Henry VIII was also a passionate man. While he surrounded himself with many of England's brilliant men, he also grew dissatisfied with all of them at some point, often to the great misfortune of those men. His court was one where the values and interests of the Renaissance were present but where they also took a backseat to larger political aspirations and ambitions.

Ultimately, the cultural renaissance that appeared briefly in Henry VIII's court was lost by Henry VIII's marriage troubles and the Reformation. These circumstances will be discussed in great detail in the next chapter, but what you need to know now is that these religious changes greatly disrupted the government and nation for many decades. Under Henry VIII, England broke with the Roman Church. Under his son, Edward VI, England became more Protestant, and under Queen Mary, England was briefly pushed back toward Catholicism. Cultural exploration and progress slowed in the face of these pressing religious issues. It was not until the reign of Elizabeth I that England settled down enough to experience its own national renaissance.

Unlike the Italian Renaissance, which was focused largely on the visual arts, England's cultural renaissance of the late 16th and early 17th centuries was far more literary. This was the era of Shakespeare, and although Shakespeare is the most well-remembered English writer from this period, he was far from the only one. John Donne, Christopher Marlowe, Ben Jonson, Edmund Spenser, and more all wrote exceptional plays and poems in this period.

What made the Elizabethan Age such a grand era for English writers, though? The English literary renaissance was, in many ways, a direct result of the Italian Renaissance. Humanism's devotion to studying humans led to the creation of more schools, and the invention of the printing press made it possible for those schools to have access to more teaching materials, such as classical texts, which before had only been accessible by an elite few. Men like Shakespeare and Marlowe were educated in these "grammar schools."

Thus, because of the impact of humanism and the Renaissance, these great English writers received a classical education that was focused largely on language. The influence this had on Shakespeare and other writers is extremely evident in the many references to classical literature in their works and their highly advanced command of the English language.

What do we mean by advanced command of the English language? The writers of that age achieved literary greatness not necessarily because of the stories they told but because of their ability to use words precisely and shape sentences eloquently. Shakespeare has not remained the most famous English writer because he came up with the story about a man who finds out his uncle murdered his father. Shakespeare didn't come up with many of his stories. He is the most famous English writer because he wrote things like "To be or not to be, that is the question." It was how Shakespeare used words that made him great, and the same can be said for many of his contemporaries. If the Italian Renaissance saw new heights of skill and expression with the paintbrush, then the English Renaissance saw the same happen with the pen.

In this discussion about the English writers' great skills during this period, it can be easy to fall into a common misconception, which is that the English Renaissance was a snobbish affair confined to the upper class. Today, we think of Shakespeare and poetry as the height of sophistication, but that was far from the case at the time. Plays were attended by all classes of society and were even viewed as scandalous and immoral by some. The writers of this time wrote about things like God and questions of morality, but they also wrote about pretty women and told dirty jokes.

The culture that these writers represented was not something confined to museums and galleries but rather something experienced by a large portion of society, which is what makes the Renaissance as a whole so important. Yes, we can spend a long time naming particular men and discussing their work, but the Renaissance was not confined to just these men. Its impact was felt directly by many through the changes it brought to education and culture, and we can still see the impact of those changes in our modern world today.

Chapter 6: The Reformation and Henry VIII

There can be no question that one of the most important events to happen in England between 1485 and 1714 was its break with the pope and the Roman Catholic Church in 1534. This event had drastic consequences at the time, and its impact shaped England for centuries to come. So, who was responsible for this momentous decision, and how exactly did it happen?

As you probably guessed from the chapter title, Henry VIII was the monarch who broke with Rome, but his reasons for doing so were far from a sense of religious conviction. It all started with Henry VIII's unfruitful marriage to Catherine of Aragon in an affair that was known as the King's Great Matter.

The King's Great Matter

The King's Great Matter was how the people of the time referred to Henry VIII's attempt to annul his marriage with Catherine of Aragon.

Catherine of Aragon by Joannes Corvus.
https://commons.wikimedia.org/wiki/File:Catalina_de_Arag%C3%B3n,_por_un_artista_an%C3%B3nimo.jpg

Catherine of Aragon was originally married to Henry's older brother, Arthur, but he died a few months after their marriage. Catherine then married Henry when he ascended to the throne in 1509. The couple appeared well matched enough until the late 1520s brought trouble in the form of Anne Boleyn.

The fact that Henry VIII simply took a liking to Anne Boleyn was not a problem for his marriage by itself. Henry VIII had already had other extramarital affairs by this point, including one with Anne's sister, Mary Boleyn. Anne, however, refused to become the king's mistress. She would not go to bed with him unless they were married.

Anne's motivation here was likely more ambition than virtue, but her stance proved to be effective. As a good Roman Catholic, Henry VIII turned to the pope to annul his marriage to Catherine so that he could marry Anne.

Anne Boleyn.
https://commons.wikimedia.org/wiki/File:AnneBoleynHever.jpg

Unfortunately for Henry VIII, the pope was not too keen on the idea. In 1527, Rome was sacked by Holy Roman Emperor Charles V. The pope was essentially Charles V's prisoner, and Charles V happened to be the nephew of Catherine of Aragon. Charles didn't like the idea of Henry VIII throwing his aunt to the side, and with his army surrounding Rome, the pope was inclined to listen to Charles V's opinion on the matter.

This dilemma went on for some time. Anne Boleyn refused to be the king's mistress. Catherine of Aragon refused to step aside. The pope refused to annul the marriage, and Henry VIII refused to give up. It went on for years, and the frustrated Henry VIII eventually began taking steps without the pope's approval. In 1531, Catherine of Aragon was kicked out of court. A year later, Henry VIII and Anne Boleyn exchanged secret vows.

However, secret vows were not enough to make Anne queen. In 1533, the highest church official in England, Thomas Cranmer, the Archbishop of Canterbury, declared Henry's marriage to Catherine of Aragon illegitimate and pronounced his marriage to Anne valid. The pope was greatly displeased, as it was clear that the English king had turned his back on Rome. In another year, the Act of Supremacy was passed by Parliament, making the king the head of the Church of England and making the break with Rome official.

Let's pause here in this real-life drama to consider a few things. First off, is it true that Henry VIII tried to get rid of his first wife and ultimately broke with Rome all because he wanted to have sex with Anne Boleyn? Anne's refusal to be the king's mistress played a role in everything that unfolded, but there was another factor that likely had a bigger influence on the king.

Catherine of Aragon was in her forties by this time, which was past childbearing years for a woman in this era. The queen had only one living child, and that child was a girl, Princess Mary. When Anne Boleyn came on the scene in the 1520s, Henry VIII had probably concluded that his current wife was not going to give him the male heir he desired. His aim in marrying Anne Boleyn was not just to fulfill his lust but also in the hopes of producing a son.

Before we judge Henry VIII too harshly, we must recognize that the lack of a male heir at this time was a very real and serious concern. At this point, England had never been ruled by a woman, and the last time a woman had been the intended heir to the throne, the country had fallen into a horrible fifteen-year civil war known as the Anarchy. None of this is to say that Henry VIII was justified in casting off his wife after almost two decades of marriage, but it does help to explain why Henry VIII was so desperate.

The next interesting thing to notice in this situation is that Henry VIII was not seeking a divorce. Although many people mistakenly say today that Henry VIII divorced three of his wives, that was not the case. Divorce back then was pretty much never allowed. Henry VIII was trying to get an annulment.

What's the difference? An annulment declares a marriage null and void. It not only ends the marriage but also renders the entire marriage invalid. If Henry VIII succeeded in gaining an annulment from Catherine of Aragon, it would be as though they were never married. Catherine would lose her title as queen, and their daughter, Princess Mary, would be considered illegitimate.

So, an annulment was serious business. Why did Henry VIII ever think the pope would grant him one? Henry VIII did have a case for his annulment, and that case rested in the Old Testament Book of Leviticus, specifically Leviticus 18:16 ("Thou shalt not uncover the nakedness of thy brother's wife: it is thy brother's nakedness") and Leviticus 20:21 ("If a man shall take his brother's wife, it is an unclean thing ... they shall be childless"). According to these verses, it appears that a man is not to marry his brother's wife. Catherine of Aragon had previously been married to Henry's brother Arthur before his death.

This issue of marrying his brother's wife had already come up. When Henry and Catherine were originally married in 1509, they had to have the pope's approval. Their marriage was only allowed because Catherine insisted that she had never consummated her marriage with Arthur, which meant that she and Arthur were never truly married. Henry VIII was hoping that the new pope would overturn that initial ruling and declare his marriage to Catherine invalid, which would allow him to marry Anne and produce a male heir.

What all this means is that the idea that Henry VIII was simply a spoiled man who changed his entire country's religion just because he had the hots for a woman isn't completely true (though it isn't completely wrong either). Henry VIII was a king without a son in a time when such circumstances often spelled disaster. He became convinced that Anne Boleyn was the key to fixing that problem.

That's how Henry VIII's marital troubles led to the establishment of the Church of England. However, none of this would have been possible had Europe not been in the midst of great religious changes in the first place. Had Henry VIII wanted to annul his marriage one hundred years prior, and the pope refused, it would have been tough luck. To truly understand why Henry VIII was able to even create the Church of England, we need to take a closer look at the religious changes that were taking place at this time.

The Reformation

The Reformation is one of the few historical movements for which we have a clear start date: October 31ˢᵗ, 1517. On this day, Martin Luther nailed his *Ninety-five Theses*, which were a collection of points of debate against the Catholic Church, to the door of a church in Wittenberg and launched a movement that would lead to a schism in the church and a long period of religious tension and even wars in Europe.

Martin Luther by Lucas Cranach the Elder.
https://commons.wikimedia.org/wiki/File:Martin_Luther,_1529.jpg

By 1517, the fact that the Catholic Church had problems with corruption was no secret. Indulgences, which was a practice that allowed people to pay off their sins, were the hot topic of the day. Luther was not the only one to take issue with indulgences. Paying off sins was a matter of utmost importance to the people who believed strongly in hell, which was practically everyone. Many of the clergy abused this fear to profit from indulgences. Luther also attacked other issues in his *Ninety-five Theses*, including church doctrine.

Luther's attack on doctrine made him different from others who had complained about the church's rampant corruption. For a long time, many had complained about corrupt clergy abusing their positions. Luther, however, went past attacking the individual clergy to debate the teachings of the church.

Still, it is unlikely that Luther could have predicted the effect his *Ninety-five Theses* would have. Such publications are normally only of interest to other theologians, but thanks to the recent invention of printing, Luther's theses spread rapidly throughout Germany, and his ideas then moved throughout Europe. The genie was out of the bottle, and the Catholic Church soon discovered that there was no putting it back.

As the name suggests, Luther's original intention was to reform the Catholic Church. He did not set out to cause a split, but the pope and other leaders in the Roman Church wanted nothing to do with Luther's suggestions. As time went on, Luther came to disagree with the Roman Church more, and the Reformation gave birth to a new sect of Christianity: Protestantism.

Luther was the spark, but many others took up the mantle of Reformation after Luther. These included men like John Knox, John Calvin, and others who would go on to found various sects of Protestantism.

It was in the backdrop of this religious upheaval that Henry VIII found himself at odds with Pope Clement VII. Many kings before Henry VIII had been frustrated by the pope's power, but Henry was the first king who was in a position to do something about it. Seventeen years after Luther published his *Ninety-five Theses*, Henry VIII started the English Reformation by breaking with the Roman Catholic Church.

The Reformation in England

Because England left the Catholic Church for political rather than religious reasons, the English Reformation was a top-down transformation. It was not the result of a change in the people's religious sentiments but rather the result of people in power making system-wide changes that trickled down to the masses. But what were these changes?

Henry VIII's Church of England was far from a radical departure from the Roman Church. Other than his denial of the pope's authority, Henry VIII appeared to hold to Catholic beliefs until his death. As such, in the new Church of England, much of the Catholic doctrine was retained, as was the general church structure with bishops and archbishops. The biggest changes were that the monarch was now head of the church instead of the pope, the monastery system was systematically extinguished, and the Bible was made available in English for the first time.

As relatively minor as these changes were, there was still resistance. Many were executed for treason in the years following the split with Rome for refusing to accept the king's supremacy over the church, including prominent men like John Fisher and Thomas More. There was also a popular uprising, the Pilgrimage of Grace, that Henry VIII thoroughly crushed. Still, for the common people, life under Henry VIII's Church of England probably did not feel that different from life under the Roman Catholic Church. Henry VIII seemed content with the few changes he had made.

Thus, the Henrician Reformation was a rather slow process whose interests were more political (the supremacy of the king) than doctrinal. Those who were executed due to Henry VIII's religious policies were often accused of treason rather than heresy. However, the English Reformation would take on a new flavor with Henry's death and the ascension of his son, Edward VI.

While Henry VIII can best be described as a Catholic who did not like the pope, Edward VI was a Protestant in name and belief. He was far more interested than his father had been in changing the people's actual beliefs, and his short six-year reign saw a much larger push toward Protestantism.

One example of this push was the Act of Uniformity passed in 1549. This act required churches to use the new English *Book of Common Prayer* written by Archbishop Cranmer. This had enormous implications for the religious lives of the English people. The *Book of Common Prayer* was used to conduct services, so the Act of Uniformity forced a great change in the weekly religious services of the common people. It was a much more substantial religious change than anything that Henry VIII had done, and it created a backlash. The Prayer Book Rebellion started in response to the Act of Uniformity and was put down by John Dudley.

Since Edward was only nine years old when he took the throne in 1547, it was men like Dudley who effectively ruled the kingdom. Dudley's success with the Prayer Book Rebellion made him essentially the most powerful man in the kingdom. He was made duke of Northumberland, and in the hopes of keeping his new power, Northumberland (Dudley) wanted to please the adolescent king.

It was this desire to stay on Edward VI's good side that likely prompted Northumberland's following actions. He greatly promoted the *Book of Common Prayer*, even getting Cranmer to write a more Protestant version in 1552. He encouraged image breaking and even the whitewashing of many ornate church walls. Under his influence, a new statement of church doctrine, the Forty-two Articles of Faith of 1553, established a more Protestant system of beliefs for the Church of England.

This was the nature of the Edwardian Reformation in England. While the Henrician Reformation had changed the church's structure, the Edwardian Reformation set out to make England Protestant in both name and belief. Catholicism was being swept away from the shores of England under the firm hand of men like Northumberland.

Unforeseen circumstances, however, soon produced a serious obstacle to this sweeping tide of Protestantism. Northumberland had bet on the wrong horse. While his radical religious stance was appreciated by Edward VI, it was heresy to others. Henry VIII's Catholic daughter Mary was next in line for the throne, and when Edward VI died in 1553, despite a brief attempt to put Lady Jane Grey on the throne, Mary became queen. Although England had been rushing toward Protestantism under Edward VI, it would soon experience religious whiplash. Queen Mary was determined to bring her country back to the Roman Catholic Church.

Unfortunately for Queen Mary, by this time, the English Reformation had effectively trickled down to the masses. Her attempts to stamp out the heresy that was Protestantism only earned her the nickname Bloody Mary. Although the English Reformation had started because of the whims of a monarch, only twenty years later, it was far too embedded in English society for anyone to turn back the tide.

Mary's attempt to make England Catholic again was brief. She died in 1558 and was replaced by her Protestant half-sister, Elizabeth. Elizabeth I's forty-four-year reign finally allowed a sense of religious stability to be established. Henry VIII had made overarching changes to the system, Edward VI had pushed drastic changes to everyday religious life, and Mary had tried to roll back these changes. Elizabeth I chose a more moderate path.

While Elizabeth restored Protestantism to England, she also firmly resisted leaning too radically into Protestantism. Despite the push for the growing sect of Puritans, the Church of England still had many resemblances to the Catholic Church. It was a church that was Protestant enough for the people of England but not Protestant enough to prompt crusades against England by Catholic nations. In this moderation, England found relative religious peace despite the religious turmoil of this period. While Henry VIII, Edward VI, and Mary had all stirred the nation, Elizabeth I allowed the nation to settle, and in doing so, she cemented the Reformation's impact on England. By the end of Elizabeth I's reign, England was Protestant, and there was no going back.

Chapter 7: Exploration and Trade

As the familiar rhyme tells us, "Columbus sailed the ocean blue in fourteen hundred ninety-two." In doing so, he inadvertently discovered a new world. The consequences of this discovery would have enormous repercussions for England and the rest of the world.

You probably already know that Columbus's discovery of the Americas was a pivotal event in world history, but there's more to this event than just its consequences. If we want to understand the nature of trade and exploration in the early modern era, we must also address the question of why Columbus was sailing the ocean blue in the first place. Columbus did not set off to find a new world. He was looking for a westward route to Asia, and the reason he was looking for such a route was quite simple: trade.

Trade in the Early Modern Era

Trade was not an invention of the early modern period. It had long been an essential part of the wealth of any city or nation. For a village to move beyond a mere subsistence existence, trade must be established to make use of surplus goods and to bring in goods only obtainable elsewhere. Trade is the very lifeblood of cities, and in the early modern period, national governments seemed to become more aware of this. Trade was how a nation could obtain great wealth—wealth that was necessary for fighting wars and maintaining defense.

The early modern era doesn't necessarily make us think of grand battles and tumultuous times in the same way the Middle Ages does, but it was a violent time nonetheless. Thanks to the Reformation, Europe was rocked by religious tensions that frequently led to armed conflicts. Dynastic conflicts also arose, as well as trade disputes. Some nations rose into world powers. Others scrambled to try to be one of those nations, and trade was their ticket.

Nations wanted power for both safety and in the hopes of dominating other nations, but power could not be had without money. And trade was where the money was. When everyone wants a piece of the action, though, there is never enough to go around. Under these circumstances, governments like Spain sent off explorers like Columbus to find new trade routes. The exploration of this period was primarily the result of the increasing importance of trade.

England and Trade

Now that we understand a bit more about trade in general in this period, let's take a closer look at English trade. As we have already mentioned, trade occurs when there is a surplus of goods that can be exchanged for something else. But how do cities and nations get enough surplus to start trading?

Specialization is the name of the game. Trade is beneficial because there are some things that a nation can easily create and other things that it can only get from other nations. For England, wool was the undisputed export king. England did not have the climate nor the landscape to make wine, silk, or grow different spices, but it did have plenty of sheep. These sheep produced wool that was then spun and made into cloth. The export of this cloth made up over three-quarters of England's exports by the start of the Elizabethan era.

Who exactly was England trading this cloth with? Their trading partners were close to home. English cloth went to cities in France and Spain, but most of all, it went to Antwerp. During the 16th century, as trade with Asia increased in importance, Antwerp became the trading hub of Europe. The majority of English cloth went there, where it was then sold and traded throughout the rest of Europe.

While England's export business was focused heavily on a single commodity, their imports were much more varied. England imported flax, wine, salt, woad (a plant used to make blue dye), spices, timber, alum, and many other goods from different countries. Surprisingly, much of what England imported came from Europe rather than from more exotic and distant locations like China. While Columbus and other explorers might make us think this period was rampant with long trade routes, at the beginning of the 16th century, much of English trade was focused within the English Channel.

Things did change over time. England's trading system took two severe hits as the early modern period progressed. The first was the lack of growth in the wool trade. Wool and the heavy cloth made from wool were close to being England's only export, and it was needed primarily by northern Europe. Eventually, there was less demand for this heavy woolen cloth. Instead of growing, English trade stagnated, and while there were attempts to fix this by developing a lighter cloth (which was called new draperies), wool prices continued to fall at the beginning of the 17th century.

The problem with the wool industry was only exacerbated by the other problem: Antwerp. Antwerp was where England sent most of its wool, but due to numerous wars, by the late 16th century, Antwerp was effectively closed to English trade. Although merchants attempted to find other locations to trade their wool, it was simply not the lucrative material it had been a century prior.

The decline of this industry was disastrous not only for the merchants but also for the government. The English government needed the money that trade brought in and was willing to intervene in the market to stop the collapse of the trade industry. The Crown's method of averting the crisis was by granting royal charters to certain companies. These charters created royal monopolies, where only those approved by the government had the right to trade in a particular area. Examples of companies created by a royal charter include the East India Company, the Virginia Company, the

Massachusetts Bay Company, the Muscovy Company, the Levant Company, and the Royal Africa Company.

Originally, these companies were formed in the hopes of finding new places to trade English wool, but many of them went on to specialize in different products. The Virginia Company was focused on tobacco. The East India Company specialized in tea, and the Royal Africa Company traded slaves. While several of these companies would go on to be enormously successful, things didn't start that way. Since we know with the benefit of hindsight that England would eventually acquire a massive empire, it can be easy to overestimate England's position in world trade in the latter half of the 16th century and into the beginning of the 17th century.

With the wool trade declining, England needed to establish alternate avenues of trade, but they were late to the party. Much of the trade with Asia was already dominated by the French and the Dutch, and Spain had already claimed huge swaths of the New World. England's late arrival forced it to begin looking for new trade routes and new lands to colonize.

Exploration

You might be thinking that because England is on an island that it has easy access to great trade routes, but that was not the case at the very beginning of the 17th century. England wasn't in the best geographical position to dive into the trade and exploration that was making countries like Spain filthy rich.

The problem was how far north England is. Attempts by the English to find northeastern or even northwestern routes to Asia ended in the ice of the North Pole. Traveling due west led English ships not to the Bahamas like Columbus but to the icy shores of Newfoundland. Despite easy access to the sea, England did not have any exclusive trade routes. Instead, England was forced to try to find a place along routes already dominated by other countries.

That is not to say the English made no contributions to the great exploratory expeditions that were going on at this time. Sir Francis Drake successfully circumnavigated the globe on a voyage from 1577 to 1580. However, Drake also used the voyage as an opportunity to harass the Spanish, making quite a bit of money with his successful pirating. Despite his piracy, Drake was welcomed back by Queen Elizabeth herself and knighted when he arrived back in England.

Drake's circumnavigation of the globe is a telling example of what most explorations boiled down to in this era: money. While circumnavigating the globe was a grand feat of human perseverance and an indication of just how much more Europeans knew about the world, it was also a money-making expedition. Drake raided the Spanish and then used the loot to purchase exotic goods, such as spices, as he traveled. We may want to believe that the spirit of adventure motivated the explorers of the early modern era, but from Columbus to Sir Francis Drake, their motivations were often more pecuniary in nature.

Trade Wars

Economics in the early modern era was more than ledger books and trade routes. There was a lot of money and power to be made and lost in international trade, and countries were willing to go to war to protect their interests.

Establishing trade routes and posts was one thing, but defending them was of equal importance. Piracy was rampant, and in India, disputes with the Dutch and French over the right to trade would escalate until the English East India Company had amassed a large army to fight its rivals. That was how intense economics was at this time. Companies had their own armies. Monopolies (which means only a single company was allowed to do business in a certain region or with a certain group) were the rule at this time, so the only way to steal business from the competition was to use force.

England was far from being a mere victim in all this. In the late 16th century, many English privateers (pirates) received implicit support from Queen Elizabeth in their raids on Spanish vessels and trading settlements. Sir Francis Drake, the famous English admiral, was among those who greatly benefited from the spoils he took from the Spanish. The English privateers harried the Spanish so much that they were a major reason for open hostilities between Spain and England from 1585 to 1604.

Sometimes, England's conflict with other nations over trade

interests went beyond piracy. England fought three wars in the latter half of the 17th century with the Dutch. Both the conflict with Spain and the conflict with the Netherlands were largely about establishing naval supremacy. The country that controlled the seas controlled trade, and as the English navy dominated the waters, England's position as a world power was secured.

However, England's success in naval warfare was not the only component in making England a dominant power. Beating its rivals in warfare was not enough to make England rich. England needed steadier and more reliable income, and it soon realized that could only be obtained with permanent settlements. Colonizing the New World was England's path to riches and power, and we will discuss how exactly that worked in Chapter 15.

The Impact of Trade and Exploration on the English People

We have discussed just how important trade and exploration were to governments in this era, but how far did this importance extend down the social ladder? Nations were becoming wealthier, but did this increase the standard of living of the average person?

The answer is not really. Trade with other nations allowed England to import new goods, but these goods were often luxury items. Silk, taffeta, and wines were brought into England in large numbers for the elite, but these luxury products were reserved for only a select few. They did little to help bolster the nation's economy as a whole.

Even the English government was aware of the problem of importing too many luxury goods instead of necessities. The Crown tried to set restrictions on the import of the elite's frivolous items, but it had little effect other than to increase smuggling. So, while trade brought money into England, that money tended to circulate amongst the upper class instead of bolstering the nation as a whole.

At this point, you may have decided that trade and exploration were nothing more than a scheme to make the rich richer and to fund wars with rival nations. However, there were some benefits beyond having cash in the treasury, and some of those benefits did impact the English people.

During the medieval period, natural disasters caused destruction on a scale that is difficult for us to fully grasp today. The Great Famine of the 14th century killed between 10 to 15 percent of the English population. In the Middle Ages, if something went wrong with the crops, there was simply nowhere else for an English peasant to get food. There was no security against the fickleness of nature.

In the early modern era, thanks to growing trade networks, there were finally alternatives to starvation when crops failed. During years of bad harvest, England was able to import grain from the Baltic, which greatly lessened the impact of crop failures. Trade did little to put more money in the pocket of the average English person, but it did help to ensure there was food at the market to buy.

Trade also brought new elements into English culture. As the early modern era went on and exploration continued, both tobacco and tea were discovered, becoming staples of English society. Sugar from the Caribbean was a prominent moneymaker for England, as well as a product that would eventually work its way into English homes everywhere. There are innumerable resources and products that came into England because of trade and forever changed the country.

By expanding what resources the country had access to, trade and exploration changed England on many levels. From necessities to interesting new products, the world was becoming increasingly interconnected, as people in different places came to rely on goods they could only obtain elsewhere. Explorations soon led to colonization as a more permanent means of securing goods. The world was changing. People were growing accustomed to what trade provided, and there was no going back.

Chapter 8: Protestantism and Its Growth

In Chapter 6, we discussed how the Reformation came to England, and we learned that the English Reformation was unique in that it was a top-down transformation where systematic changes enacted by those in power altered the country's religion. In this chapter, we look to address a slightly different question: how did Protestantism come to England?

While the Reformation and Protestantism might seem like the same thing, there is a difference. The Reformation was a reactionary movement to the people's problems with the Catholic Church. It began as an attempt to reform the Catholic Church but instead led to the establishment of Protestantism.

Protestantism is the belief system (or rather belief systems because there are many different sects) that arose as a direct result of the Reformation. It moved beyond criticizing Catholicism to having a different and opposing set of doctrinal beliefs. What this means in England particularly is that the Reformation was a series of systematic changes to religious forms and practices, but Protestantism was a change to doctrine and belief itself.

The Reformation and Protestantism are closely tied together, and in many cases, discussing them as if they were practically the same causes no harm. However, England is a unique case. Although

Henry VIII did undoubtedly bring the Reformation to England, he did not make great efforts to bring Protestantism along with it. Henry VIII was a Catholic who denied the pope's authority. He was not a true Protestant in any sense of the word. However, in bringing the Reformation to England, Henry VIII had opened a door, and Protestantism would soon follow.

Catholicism vs. Protestantism

To understand how Protestantism came to and impacted England, we first need to understand what the difference between Catholicism and Protestantism was. If denying the pope's authority didn't make Henry VIII a full Protestant, what did?

The main difference between Catholicism and Protestantism at this time lay in where they found the truth. Catholics saw divine revelation in the Bible, church tradition, and church authority. Although the Bible was considered to be God's Word, for Catholics, the average person could not be trusted to interpret it. The clergy was responsible for telling the people what the Bible said, and in doing so, they became sources of truth. Protestantism, however, saw the Bible alone as the source of truth. The clergy and church tradition should only be followed when they agreed with scripture.

Because Protestants believed in the authority of scripture alone, they thought it was important for everyone to be able to read the Bible. This led to the first English translation of the Good Book. The denial of the clergy as sources of truth also meant that the Protestants viewed priests differently. Priests were not sacred to Protestants, so their role became less about performing sacraments and more about preaching. Protestants even rejected the idea that the Eucharist was transformed into the literal body and blood of Christ because that had the priest performing a supernatural miracle.

What these differences culminated in and what made the debate between Catholics and Protestants so momentous was ultimately a different path to heaven. Catholicism believed that salvation was the product of both faith and good works. To get to heaven, one not only needed to believe, but one also needed to do what the church said by engaging in the sacraments. Protestantism saw faith alone as the way to salvation. The path to heaven was a matter of personal belief, and a priest or the church could do nothing to put someone on that path.

These differences between Catholicism and Protestantism quickly created a chasm. To Catholics, Protestantism was heresy. It denied the authority of God's church and God's spokesman on Earth, the pope. To Protestants, Catholicism was blasphemous in suggesting that Christ's redemptive work on the cross needed assistance from humans in the form of good works. There was no reconciling the two, and the tension between them led to many conflicts, both on an individual and national scale.

Sliding into Protestantism

Now that we have a better idea of just what everyone was so upset about, let's return to the question of Protestantism in England. When Henry VIII broke with Rome, he denied the authority of the pope. As we have seen from the differences between Catholicism and Protestantism, rejecting the clergy's authority, particularly the pope, was to deny the source of truth itself. Henry VIII had led England down a slippery slope, and now it was just a matter of how fast the country would slide down it.

One of the big questions we must stop and ask at this point is just what everyone else was thinking at this time. Sure, Henry VIII had marital troubles, and he didn't like the pope telling him what to do, but he had to get Parliament to agree to break with Rome and create the Church of England.

The fact that Henry VIII does not appear to have had much trouble getting his nobles to agree to leave the Catholic Church indicates that Protestantism had at least some roots in England before the break with Rome. These Protestant sympathies among the ruling classes became more obvious after the break. People like Thomas Cromwell, Thomas Cranmer, and even Anne Boleyn tried to push Henry VIII toward more Protestant ideas. However, the king still considered himself a good Catholic, and other powerful people wanted him to stay that way. In some ways, the English court after the break with Rome was a microcosm of the religious tensions in Europe, as those with Catholic and Protestant sympathies sought to influence the king.

However, the debate between Catholicism and Protestantism would not be solved in Henry VIII's lifetime. Henry VIII never really leaned into Protestant doctrine, but as long as he denied the pope's authority, Catholicism wasn't truly an option either. The English court would continue to oscillate between Protestantism and Catholicism for the next several decades until Elizabeth I.

The Dissolution of the Monasteries

The English elite were made up of both Catholic and Protestant sympathizers, all of whom were trying to ensure that the king or queen was on their side. But how did the common people feel about all of this? Perhaps the best place to illustrate the difference between the move toward Protestantism in the upper and lower classes is with the dissolution of the monasteries.

Monasteries were a unique institution in the medieval and early modern era. They often served a critical role in the local area, acting as schools and hospitals, but as religious institutions, they were independent (not under the control of the government). When Henry VIII became the head of the Church of England, effectively combining the government and church, something had to be done with the eight hundred or so religious houses in England.

The natural solution seemed to be to fold the monasteries into the new religious system. This meant the monasteries had to accept the king's supremacy. In making himself head of all the monasteries, Henry VIII also made himself the owner of all monastic properties in England, which was no small amount. At this time, monasteries owned around a fourth of all the worked land in England. It was a very tempting acquisition for Henry VIII.

Still, it was not immediately obvious that the government intended to dissolve the monasteries. Things began with Henry VIII sending out commissioners, overseen by Thomas Cromwell, to visit and value the various monasteries. The information-gathering expeditions proved to be quite the ordeal. The government lacked the infrastructure to perform such a task satisfactorily, and the previously independent monasteries did not react well to the government sticking its nose in their business. However, Cromwell was a determined man, and despite setbacks, the commissioners completed several circuits of the kingdom's monasteries in the years following the break with Rome.

For a time, it appeared that the government's great interest in the monasteries would lead to reform. However, in 1536, the first Act of Suppression was passed, and the writing was on the wall. All monasteries whose income amounted to less than two hundred pounds a year were to be dissolved. Their possessions and land were to be taken by the Crown.

As you can imagine, many monasteries did not react well to this. There were widespread attempts to destroy monastic property and thus rob the Crown of its gain. Some monasteries were aided in this attempt by the local populace, while others found the locals took the opportunity to help themselves to monastic property. The reaction against the dissolution of the monasteries was so strong that it resulted in an uprising in the north.

The Pilgrimage of Grace, as it came to be known, was thoroughly and swiftly crushed by Henry VIII, but it did show there was an adverse reaction to the reforms amongst the general population. Monasteries played vital roles in communities. They were a place for the sick to seek treatment, for boys to receive some education, and even for the poor to seek shelter. Dissolving them was a noticeable disruption to local life, which caused some to protest against the top-down reformation that Henry VIII's government had imposed on England. It was clear that whatever Henry VIII's government had decided, the people of England were still attached to their old religious institutions.

However, the Pilgrimage of Grace did nothing to halt the changing tides. In 1539, the Second Act of Suppression was passed, which allowed for the dissolution of larger monasteries. By 1541, all of the monasteries in England had been dissolved.

The nobles of English society showed far less discontent than the working class had at this decision, and that was most likely because they benefited from it. Henry VIII gifted monastic lands to his supporters, which was a very simple and effective way to ensure that more of the upper class were at least outwardly embracing the religious changes. With the dissolution of the monasteries, England was sliding closer and closer to Protestantism, and the lower classes were being pulled along for the ride.

Habit and Belief

With moves like the dissolution of monasteries, the common people found their lives irrevocably changed, and there was unrest. The Pilgrimage of Grace in 1536 is one such example, as is the Prayer Book Rebellion of 1549. It is clear from these examples that England was not wholly Protestant in belief, but at some point, that attitude changed. By the time James II took the throne in 1685, the English people could not stomach the thought of a Catholic king. What changed? How did the English go from having Protestantism forced on them by Henry VIII and Edward VI to despising James II for being Catholic?

One reason may simply be nothing more than the nature of religion in this period. Today, we view religion as a choice, not only in whether you want to be religious or not but also in the myriad of different religious options available. In early modern England, religion was not a choice. Everyone was religious, and all of the churches were essentially the same. There was no going down the street to a different church if you didn't like the way your church conducted worship. Religion was a national affair, and everyone across the country was pretty much part of the same church.

This meant that whatever your personal beliefs, thanks to Henry VIII and the Reformation, you were now worshiping in a Protestant service. And as they say, habit builds character. Changing how the English people worshiped and even what they were taught in services were bound to eventually change their beliefs as well.

Since most people had little access to religious information outside of what their local priest told them, this transition likely occurred faster and smoother than we might anticipate since people simply followed the guidance of their local priest. Centuries of medieval Catholicism had trained the majority of people to follow the clergy, and ironically, that might have made England's transition to Protestantism easier. The top-down style of the English Reformation was effective partially because the old Catholic religious system already had a hierarchical structure in place. Protestantism was spread simply by changing the people at the top of this structure.

Fear of Popery

Of course, the problem with discussing the spread of Protestantism is that we are dealing with a matter of personal belief. We know that the English people were forced to act more Protestant through the changes instilled by their government, but it's very difficult to track what exactly this did to the average person's beliefs.

However, we can get a sense of just how Protestant England was becoming through external events. We know that England was truly becoming Protestant because of the rising fear of popery.

Until the 1534 break with Rome, England was Roman Catholic. After that, England's relationship with the Roman Catholic Church began to deteriorate. When Queen Mary took the throne and tried to push the nation back toward Catholicism, it only worsened the English people's opinion of Catholics. Mary burned around three hundred Protestants at the stake, and many more fled the country during her reign. Propaganda after Mary's death only served to worsen Mary's image and the overall view of Catholics.

The next major strike against Catholics in the English mind was the Gunpowder Plot of 1605. The Gunpowder Plot was a conspiracy hatched by some English Roman Catholics to blow up Parliament and kill the new king, James I.

Nothing makes paranoia worse than a real conspiracy. The Gunpowder Plot made Catholics the worst sort of villains in the eyes of the English people. To this day, people in England burn effigies of Guy Fawkes on November 5th every year. With the Gunpowder Plot, mistrust and fear of popery (Catholicism) were beginning to become part of the English culture.

England's Protestant government saw no reason to check this growing paranoia, and by 1678, it had reached its peak. In that year, a man named Titus Oates created a story that Jesuits were planning to assassinate Charles II and put his Catholic brother James on the throne. The conspiracy was entirely made up, but it resulted in dozens of arrests and even executions. It took years before the government was able to see through Oates's story, despite the fact that Titus Oates was an incredibly untrustworthy character with a bad reputation.

The success of the fabricated Popish Plot in stirring up England against Catholics demonstrates just how much the country was steeped in Protestantism. Distrust of Catholics was almost part of being English. The hostility against a common enemy united the English people and even helped contribute to a growing sense of nationalism. When James II, who was a known Catholic, took the throne, he never stood a chance.

In 1553, Mary was able to hold the throne until her death, despite being Catholic and even ordering the deaths of Protestants. By 1665, James II was king for only three years before being forced to flee. In the century between these two Catholic rulers, England had changed. While we may not be able to tell exactly at what point many English people accepted Protestantism, we can tell from the rising dislike of popery that it had become widely accepted. Catholicism was out, and Protestantism was there to stay.

The Puritans

To close this chapter on Protestantism in England, we should take a moment to ask ourselves just how Protestant England was. You might be thinking, based on their hatred of Catholics, that England was strictly Protestant, but that was far from the case. The Anglican Church or the Church of England was in many ways similar to the Catholic Church.

Understanding just where England fell on the Protestant spectrum may be most easily understood by looking at a smaller group within England's religious scene: the Puritans. Their name comes from the fact that they wanted to purify the Church of England by removing all Roman Catholic practices. The fact that such a group existed in the first place tells you already that the Church of England was not at the extreme end of Protestantism.

The Puritans were a rather outspoken group throughout the 16th and 17th centuries, and because of this, they were a source of frustration to the monarch. Puritans wanted the Church of England to be far more reformed, and there were enough of them in Parliament that Elizabeth I had to hear about it constantly. However, Elizabeth I was determined to stick with her moderate religious settlement, and the Puritans were repressed though not eliminated.

They continued to be an outspoken group in England, reaching the height of their influence during the Interregnum when Oliver Cromwell, who was a Puritan, ruled England as Lord Protector. After the English Restoration, though, England's patience with the Puritans sharply declined. Many Puritans, realizing they would never be able to create the pure religious state that they wanted in England, moved to try their experiment in the American colonies.

What this extremely brief history of the Puritans demonstrates is that England never fully embraced the more radical versions of Protestantism that were taking hold in places like Geneva and Germany. Starting with the break with Rome in 1534, England slipped further from Catholicism into Protestantism, but where they ultimately landed was fairly close to the middle.

Chapter 9: Law(s) and Order

Some things never change. No matter the time or the place, crime and disorder are something that every society has to find ways of dealing with. However, the way in which different societies at different times deal with issues of law and order varies greatly.

In the 16th and 17th centuries, law and order in England looked very different than it does now. If someone broke into your house, there were no police to call. If a riot broke out in the city of London, there was no standing army to put it down. If you were arrested, there was no jail to send you to as punishment. Maintaining peace and punishing offenders had to be achieved through different means than what we rely on today. Some of those means may seem strange or even brutal, while others may appear quite close to our modern procedures.

Common Law vs. Statutory Law

Before getting into specific laws and procedures for dealing with crime, we first need to discuss the basic breakdown of English law in this period. By the early modern era, English law was made up of both common law and statutory law.

Common law has been around since the Early Middle Ages and refers to law based on custom. Common law uses previous cases and decisions to decide the proper course of action in new cases. Before the existence of a written legal code, common law was the only thing keeping the English judicial system coherent and consistent.

Statutory law refers to written laws, such as acts of Parliament. In England, statutory law did not come into existence until Edward I's reign in the late 13th century. This was the first time that legislation was written down that both amended and clarified common law.

While we often think of the law as being a set of written rules (which would be statutory law), both English and American law to this day rely heavily on common law. Following common law means that we expect the court to refer back to previous cases and to act consistently in the way in which the law is interpreted. Then, when a court decides on a particular case, they are adding to common law. Courts do not create new laws, but how they rule sets a precedent, and that precedent is part of common law.

The early modern era was crucial for both common and statutory law. For common law, this period saw a much greater emphasis on documentation. Although common law is based on custom rather than statutes, the lack of a written record leaves far too much room for abuses. There is little that cannot be claimed when referring to an abstract body of legal tradition.

Writing down the already existing common law was of vast importance, and a man named Sir Edward Coke did much of this. In his four-volume *Institutes of the Lawes of England*, Coke examined what common law said about various legal matters, creating a much-needed and concise documentation of common law. Coke also aided common law in his eleven-volume *Reports*, which was a collection of court cases with Coke's commentary.

These books became important references for others since they were a valuable resource for clarifying just what the common law's customs were. Since common law is based on precedent, having records of those precedents is crucial.

Acts of Parliament

Of course, the early modern period also saw changes to statutory law, meaning it saw the creation of entirely new laws. While judges and courts are the ones who create common law through their interpretations and precedents, legislators are the ones who create statutory law.

Parliament was certainly busy during the 229 years of the early modern period, and we can't even begin to discuss all of the laws it passed. However, we will look at four particular acts of Parliament to get a better idea of what statutory law includes and how it was used in England at this time.

- Poor Law: The Poor Law refers to numerous laws passed in the Elizabethan era that were designed to address the growing problem of poverty. These laws gave responsibility for the poor to parishes. Parishes were to provide aid to the sick, infants, disabled, and elderly and provide work for the able-bodied poor, resulting in the creation of workhouses. We will learn more about why England faced a poverty problem and just how effective these relief efforts were in Chapter 11.

- Book of Sports: The Book of Sports was a declaration made by James I in 1618, which permitted recreational activities on Sunday. The Puritan reaction against this order was so strong that James I was forced to withdraw it. Charles I reinstated it, despite the still vocal opposition, in 1633, but it was overturned during the Interregnum and not made legal again until the English Restoration in 1660.

- Clarendon Code: The Clarendon Code, so-called because it was passed during the ministry of Edward Hyde (the Earl of Clarendon), was a series of four acts passed from 1661 to 1665 that attacked the Nonconformists or Dissenters. Nonconformists were Protestants who did not adhere to the beliefs and practices of the Church of England. The Corporation Act, the Act of Uniformity, the Conventicle Act, and the Five Mile Act did everything from excluding Nonconformists from holding church offices to making it illegal for them to worship. Essentially, the code was designed to make it impossible to be a Nonconformist in England.

- Toleration Act: The Clarendon Code proved to be ineffective in wiping out Nonconformists. Twenty-four years later, the Toleration Act was passed. This act granted freedom of worship to Nonconformists. They still faced legal discrimination in other areas, such as being unable to hold political office, but they could now have their own churches and preachers.
- These four acts of Parliament give a brief glimpse of what the lawmakers of the early modern period were interested in regulating. Many of the major acts of this time were focused on religion, which was a product of both the English government's new jurisdiction over religious matters following the break with Rome and the high religious tensions of the day. Creating the Church of England had combined the state and church, and the state was trying to figure out what aspects of religion they could control.

What stands out about statutory law in the early modern era was its readiness to regulate morality. In the phrase "law and order," we reveal our own modern mindset that the purpose of the law is to maintain order. However, in early modern England, there was more of a willingness to go beyond that purpose. Laws like the Book of Sports and the Clarendon Code are not necessarily about keeping order but more about guiding the people toward certain values and a particular religion. In the cases of both of these laws, though, the government soon learned that policing the people's morals and beliefs is practically impossible.

The Toleration Act is a clear sign that England was beginning to accept that trying to force a perfectly uniform religion on its people would never lead to lasting peace. Using the law to control people's personal beliefs simply does not work. The Toleration Act was still a long way off from religious freedom, but we can see a slight shift from laws regulating beliefs to a law that makes concessions to maintain order. This shift would continue over time, but even today, it is far from fully settled. Governments still struggle with finding the line in what laws can and cannot regulate about citizens' behavior.

Crime in Early Modern England

We have talked at length about the law, but that's only half the picture. To understand the state of overall order in early modern England, we also have to look at crime.

One assumption that many people make unwittingly is that violent crimes were rampant. After all, this was a time when dueling and fistfights were acceptable ways to settle a conflict. It was also a time when most people went around armed in some fashion. It seems like a recipe for a society to be torn apart by violence.

Surprisingly, this was not the case. Records from the day show that premeditated murder was rare. The majority of violent crimes were spontaneous, erupting as drunken brawls or in the heat of a dispute. However, even these spontaneous acts of violence were far from being the majority of criminal activity. That honor goes to a different class of crime.

Property offenses were by far the dominant crime in early modern England. Property-based crimes made up well over half of the court cases. Your stuff getting stolen was far more likely than you getting stabbed.

To some degree, the large degree of theft makes perfect sense. As we discussed in Chapter 7 on trade and exploration, the rich were getting richer, but this was not trickling down to the lower classes. The gap was only made more visible by population spikes that led to an ever-growing number of impoverished people. It should not come as a surprise that in a society where poverty was increasing, theft was common.

However, we should be careful in using this explanation of class warfare to account for all property offenses. Not all property offenses involved a poor person taking from a rich person. The lower classes also stole from each other, and neighbors of the same class were willing to take each other to court over these crimes, indicating that stealing was viewed as a punishable offense by virtually everyone. Even though it is likely that the economic realities did have an impact on the prevalence of theft, this was not a society embroiled in secret class warfare where the poor cheered each other on as they took from the rich.

Speaking of class warfare, some crimes did point to the struggle between the classes far more clearly. Rioting was fairly common and used by the lower classes to express their displeasure with a particular issue, such as an increase in food prices.

What is strange about rioting in this period is that it seems to have been a generally accepted safety valve through which the lower classes were allowed to vent their frustrations. While the government tended to react harshly against rebellions, which were organized political revolts, its reaction to riots was relatively lax. The hierarchical feudal system of the Middle Ages was disappearing, but there was still a paternalistic sense of duty that existed between the upper and lower classes. Lords were supposed to care for those under them, and the lower classes saw riots, despite their illegality, as a legitimate way of reminding the elite of their duty.

Another way in which crime often showed a difference between the upper and lower classes was in the area of moral offenses. Things like adultery and drunkenness were not only frowned upon but illegal. The punishments for such offenses typically involved public humiliation, such as being paraded through the streets or whipped in the square, to discourage such behavior.

In general, the lower classes were far less likely to drag someone to court over these types of offenses. For example, the elite attempted to outlaw unregulated alehouses because they viewed them as dens that bred immorality. However, the lower classes had no problem with their neighbors drinking wherever they chose, so the law against unregulated alehouses was virtually unenforceable.

Therefore, in certain moral offenses, we can see a sharp divide between the attitudes of the classes. What the wealthy viewed as criminal, the poor might view as a mere nuisance or entirely harmless. The lack of agreement on these types of offenses made enforcing them extremely difficult. The elite's attempt to police the lower class's morality was often a fruitless endeavor that showed just how necessary consistency is to the power of the law.

Enforcing the Law

We have talked about how people broke the law, but what happened after someone broke it? As we mentioned earlier in this chapter, jail time was not a common form of punishment. Jails in this period were simply used to hold those awaiting trial. They were not a way to punish offenders.

The biggest detriment of how the law was enforced in early modern England was the victim. As long as there were no deaths, the victim was the one who chose whether to get the law involved. Since punishments were harsh, there were instances of people working out their issues without resorting to a court decision.

If the victim decided to report the matter, they would inform the constable, whose responsibility was to investigate and make the arrest. However, the constable was a part-time position, so there was a real possibility that while the constable was trying to do this, the accused could catch wind of everything and flee.

If the accused were arrested, they were brought before the judge. At this point, if the victim wanted to prosecute the accused, they had to pay prosecuting costs. If the judge and victim agreed on the charge, an indictment would be created. A grand jury would then meet and decide whether the case went to court or if the indictment would be thrown out. If it went to court, the case would be tried before a jury, which determined innocence or guilt. The judge was the one who passed the sentence.

What this perhaps tedious explanation of the justice system shows us is two things. One, the early modern justice system has a lot in common with many justice systems today. Trial by jury was the standard, although it would be a while before that jury included anyone other than landowning white men.

Two, there were a lot of steps in the process, and all of those steps left the accused with many places to get out of trouble. Punishments were harsh. Stealing goods valued at over one shilling was a hangable offense, but we should not assume that meant early modern people were hanging everyone who stole a piece of bread. Even for those who made it all the way through the process and were found guilty by the jury, less than half were sentenced to death by the judge. Justice in early modern England was not that sadistic.

Then, why were the punishments so harsh? Remember, there were no police. There was no system for crime prevention. Enforcing the law was strictly regulated to punishing criminals. Punishments were harsh because this was seen as the only viable way to deter crime. The only way to stop someone from stealing was to make sure they were more afraid of what would happen if they were caught.

Accusations of Witchcraft

We have so far explored an overview of crime, law, and order in early modern England, but before we end the chapter, let's take the time to look at one of the most bizarre aspects of law and order in this period: witchcraft.

Despite what the movie *Monty Python and the Holy Grail* implies, accusations against witches were not common in the Middle Ages. In the Middle Ages, they didn't even have any laws outlawing witchcraft. Parliament passed the first law making witchcraft a crime punishable by death in 1542, but the law was repealed just five years later. It was not until 1562 that it was restored. Things soon started to get out of hand.

For around eighty years in England, starting in the 1560s, accusations and prosecutions of alleged witches skyrocketed. One instance in Pendle in 1612 saw twelve people from two families accused of witchcraft. Of the twelve, one died while awaiting trial, and ten were found guilty and executed. Only one of the accused escaped with their life.

There has been a myriad of attempts to explain this sudden and unprecedented rise in the accusation and prosecution of witches. Some historians have connected it to the religious changes brought on by the Reformation, but that does not necessarily explain why the accused tended to fit the witch stereotype, typically being old, poor, single, and female. Feminists argue that it was the result of patriarchal society's attempts to exercise power and control over women, but this explanation does not seem to explain why women often accused other women or why this phenomenon occurred at this particular time. English society had been sexist (at least by our standards) for a long time.

In the case of the Pendle witches, there appear to have been multiple factors at play. Some of the accused did confess to believing in their own powers, and there was a rivalry between two families that likely fueled the accusations. Prior illnesses and deaths in the village were used as evidence, and a nine-year-old child was allowed to act as a key witness (something that was not allowed in English courts back then for any crime other than witchcraft). If the Pendle witch trial is anything to go on, it is hard and likely incorrect to point to a single reason as the definitive explanation for this strange phenomenon.

The eighty years in which witchcraft trials exploded serves as a grim reminder that while the early modern period was the time of the Renaissance and many advancements, superstition still abounded. The narrative that this period left behind the dark ignorance of the Middle Ages does not tell the whole story. We should be wary of any historical explanation that acts as those a country makes nothing but uphill progress. Accusing people of witchcraft was not a problem in the Middle Ages. It was a uniquely early modern phenomenon.

Chapter 10: Revolution and Rebellion

Early modern England was nothing if not a time of change. The Reformation produced religious changes that rippled outward, impacting all levels of society. Exploration introduced new products and brought in new wealth. The Renaissance widened the scope of education and caused innovation in the arts and sciences. The overall population was growing, and the importance of urban areas was increasing as England slowly began to move from an agrarian to an industrial society.

All of those changes created the England we know today, but if there's one thing we all know about change, it is that's it hard. England was a pot that was constantly being stirred, which created quite a bit of agitation. A time rife with change was also rife with revolutions and rebellions. Here are some of the most interesting and most important ones from the early modern era.

The Cornish Rebellion (1497)

Cornwall has always had a strong sense of identity and autonomy, and the Cornish Rebellion of 1497 is a potent example of that.

It was twelve years after the Wars of the Roses. Henry VII's grip on the throne was relatively secure, but there were those who were not ready to completely give up the Yorkist claim. The problem was a man named Perkin Warbeck. Warbeck claimed to be Richard, Duke of York, one of the princes who had been imprisoned in the Tower of London by their uncle, Richard III, and then presumably killed. Warbeck's story wasn't convincing, but he managed to gain the support of James IV of Scotland, who supported Warbeck as the rightful claimant to the English throne, likely because he wanted to cause trouble for Henry VII and England.

With James IV's support, Warbeck became a real threat, and Henry VII had to deal with him. However, this was happening in Scotland in the north. What does it have to do with Cornwall? Fighting wars takes money, and as one of the measures to raise money, Henry VII raised taxes in Cornwall.

As much as we don't like the government raising taxes today, in 1497, it was even worse. A centralized government was still a relatively new concept. The idea that the government could take money from people in one region to deal with a problem in a separate region was strange, and the Cornish people didn't like it.

Still, that might not have pushed them over the edge if Henry VII hadn't added another insult: dissolving the Stannary Parliament. Tin mining was so big in Cornwall that it had its own law and government institution: the Stannary Parliament. Although the Stannary Parliament was not technically a national assembly (it only controlled tin mining), so many people in Cornwall were involved in tin mining that it was a powerful institution and gave Cornwall a sense of autonomy. Thus, Henry VII dissolving it was a slap in the face to the Cornish. Adding that to the new taxes was enough to push the region over the edge.

The angry Cornish rebels soon amassed around fifteen thousand people. They were enough of a threat for Henry VII to leave his conflict with Scotland and bring his forces south to deal with the uprising. The two sides faced off outside London at the Battle of Blackheath on June 17th, 1497.

The outcome was almost inevitable. The rebels were outnumbered and had no military experience or leadership. The king's forces crushed them. However, despite losing the battle, the Cornish got what they wanted. Henry VII brought back the Stannary Parliament, and he never tried to tax Cornwall so highly again.

Because the rebellion was fairly successful in its aims, the Cornish Rebellion of 1497 is seen as a high point for Cornwall. To this day, the region continues to maintain a sense of independence and identity.

The Prayer Book Rebellion and Kett's Rebellion (1549)

The Prayer Book Rebellion and Kett's Rebellion are two popular uprisings that occurred in different regions of England around the same time in 1549.

The Prayer Book Rebellion, as the name implies, started because of the *Book of Common Prayer*. Parliament had passed the Act of Uniformity, which required the new English prayer book to be used. In the west of England, the common people did not take kindly to this and began to demand that the services be returned to Latin.

The unrest caused by the changes to religious services was only made worse by the economic problems. The population was growing faster than the economy could adjust. There were too many people and not enough jobs and resources. These economic problems caused another rebellion to break out in the north of Norfolk.

Kett's Rebellion began as a riot when Robert Kett enclosed his land. Enclosure was when the English gentry seized control of common land, which was available for use by everyone. You can imagine why enclosing land made so many people angry, especially during times of economic hardship. Common land was often the only land those further down the social ladder had access to.

Enclosure riots were extremely common in this period, but what was remarkable about the one in Norfolk in 1549 was that Robert Kett listened. He agreed with the rioters. He joined them and ended up leading a mass of rebels. The rebels were even able to capture the city of Norwich and sent a list of demands to the government, which included moderate requests like reducing rent and radical ones like ending private land ownership.

While one rebellion was more religious in nature and one more economic, the fact that both the Prayer Book Rebellion and Kett's Rebellion broke out around the same time shows just how tense this time was. Religious changes and economic problems were putting a strain on the English people, and the pot was starting to boil over.

Ultimately, the pot did not boil completely because both rebellions were put down similarly: they were put down brutally. John Dudley used the rebellions as a chance to seize power. He dealt with both Kett's Rebellion in the north and the Prayer Book Rebellion in the west by raising an army and swiftly crushing the rebels. By doing this, he proved his ability to maintain order and became the de facto leader of the country until Edward VI's death.

Such effective crushing of popular uprisings was typical of the Tudor era. While the people's grievances were often reasonable, the dissolution of order could not be allowed. This strict attitude may have kept England from dissolving into something more chaotic during the chaos of the Reformation.

The English Civil War (1642–1651)

The English Civil War had some drastic consequences. It ended with the execution of a king and led to eleven years where England was without a king (the Interregnum). But what started it in the first place?

As we discussed in Chapter 3, Charles I was a king who believed greatly in his power. However, by the 1600s, Parliament had been around for over four hundred years, and its members were used to having the monarchs heed their advice.

The sticking point, as usual, was war and money. Monarchs wage wars, but wars cost money, and under the English governing system, taxes could only be raised with Parliament's consent. By the late 1620s, Parliament had had enough of war (at least enough of Charles I's wars because he kept losing). There were several disagreements between Charles I and Parliament at this time, but it culminated in a dramatic ending of Parliament in 1629.

Parliament and Charles I were in open disagreement. Charles I again wanted money to fight wars, but Parliament did not want to give it to him. Seeing that he was getting nowhere, Charles I decided to dissolve Parliament, but this time, the assembly refused to go quietly. Parliament was adjourned when the speaker of the House of Commons announced the adjournment and rose from his chair. When the speaker tried to rise and adjourn the House on March 2nd, 1629, several members of Parliament forcibly held him down so that the House could pass three further resolutions, all of which condemned Charles I's actions. It was an open and clear statement that Parliament did not believe it existed to do the king's bidding. Charles I was furious. He would not call another meeting of Parliament during the next eleven years.

The eleven-year period in which Charles I tried to rule without Parliament is known as the Personal Rule, and it required Charles I to get quite creative. Running a country takes money. The typical way governments get that money is through taxation, and only Parliament could approve taxes. To meet his financial needs without the ability to levy taxes, Charles I relied on a combination of stricter budgeting and several other creative methods, such as selling monopolies, collecting fines, and leveraging taxes from laws that were long forgotten but still technically on the books.

This was not enough. Scotland rebelled, and Charles I had to have money to raise an army. In the spring of 1640, Charles I called Parliament again. Parliament, however, was not about to give Charles I the money he wanted to raise an army. After eleven years of Personal Rule, Parliament did not trust Charles I. When it became clear that Parliament was not going to give Charles I what he wanted, he dissolved the assembly after only three short weeks, giving this event the nickname of the Short Parliament.

Dismissing Parliament did not solve Charles I's problems, though. Scotland was still in rebellion and making advances in the north of England. Without money, Charles I could not raise a royal army to stop the Scottish invasion. London itself was wide open, so later that same year (1640), Charles I was forced to call Parliament yet again. This time, the meeting would be much longer.

When the Long Parliament first met, the vast majority of the assembly was in agreement that Charles I had gone too far. A man named John Pym emerged as the leader of this huge majority, and Parliament began passing bills to reform the king's policies. With the threat of Scotland hanging over him, Charles I was forced to agree. As time went on, though, the bills became more and more radical. Parliament began to lose its unified front against the king as conservatives and then moderates began to think that Pym and his party were going too far. While they might have disagreed with the king's policies, many still did not question his right to rule, and the attacks on royal power were losing support.

By the end of 1641, Parliament, which had been firmly united at the beginning of 1640, was split in two. When Pym introduced the Grand Remonstrance, which was a list of grievances with the king, Pym's radical group barely won the vote, with the final count being 158 to 149. Parliament and the country were split into two groups: Royalists and Parliamentarians. Royalists believed the king should still be the practical ruler, while Parliamentarians wanted to push the government toward a constitutional monarchy.

At this time, with the country now split down the middle, Ireland rebelled. With both Scotland and Ireland up in arms, England needed an army, but for either Parliament or the king to raise one would be seen as a threat by the other side. Trust between the Royalist side and the Parliamentarian side had deteriorated to such a degree that there was no longer a path forward. Each side armed itself, and when Charles I raised his banner on August 22nd, 1642, the English Civil War began.

We do not have the space here to dive into the military details of this conflict, but the hostilities lasted for around nine years. The main conflict between the forces of Charles I (nicknamed the Cavaliers) and the Parliamentarians (nicknamed the Roundheads due to their short-cropped hair) lasted for around four years, from 1642 to 1646. While the Cavaliers did well at the beginning of the conflict, they were unable to capture London, without which it was impossible to bring a true end to the conflict. During this time, Oliver Cromwell rose as a competent military leader of the Roundheads.

Cromwell at the Battle of Naseby by Charles Landseer.
https://commons.wikimedia.org/wiki/File:Charles_Landseer_Cromwell_Battle_of_Naseby.JPG

The turning point was the Battle of Naseby (June 14th, 1645). Here, the Roundheads won a decisive victory, and fortune turned against the Cavaliers. Royalist forces continued to lose battles, and with the help of the Scottish, Parliament defeated the king's forces by 1646.

Now, what should happen at this point was clear to everyone involved. This was not the first time disagreements between the monarch and the ruling elite had come to blows. Barons and kings had fought against each other in the medieval period, and when the king lost such conflicts, the normal procedure was for the king to make concessions. Beating the king in a war meant he had to agree to the winners' demands. It did not mean that he stopped being king.

In 1646, this is what everyone expected to happen. Charles I had lost, and he would have to do at least some of what the Parliamentarians wanted. However, Charles I decided that he would make no concessions. Despite having lost the war and being under house arrest, Charles I believed so strongly in his own sovereignty that he refused to negotiate with the victors. Efforts to speak to the king and reach an agreement lasted for three years. Finally, in 1649, Parliament turned to drastic measures. Charles I was tried for treason and executed. England had killed its king.

The fighting dragged on after the execution of Charles I, lasting until around 1652. Both Ireland and Scotland chose to support Charles II, Charles I's son, but Cromwell and his army were able to defeat all opponents. When Charles II fled to France in 1651, the hostilities ended. The English Civil War was over, and England had overthrown its king.

We know with the benefit of hindsight that this situation did not last. England was without a king for eleven years, during which time Oliver Cromwell ruled as Lord Protector. Once Cromwell died, England found itself unsure how to proceed, and Charles II was invited back. The monarchy was restored in 1660.

Because the monarchy was restored, many people today overlook the English Civil War when considering the end of the monarchy and the beginning of democracy in Europe. We often look to the American and French Revolutions as the beginning of the end of monarchy, but a century before those revolutions, England had proven there was indeed a limit to how far a king could exercise his power.

The fact that England restored its monarchy after this tumultuous period simply shows that there was still relatively little understanding or thought put into what an alternate government would look like. Under Cromwell, England's government was far closer to a constitutional monarchy than a republic. Nevertheless, the English Civil War is important. It would spark a century of thinking and political philosophy that would provide the foundation for the later American and French Revolutions.

The Glorious Revolution (1688–1689)

What makes a revolution glorious? Is it the fight for a noble cause? Is it a bloody overthrow of a tyrannical government? Is it the upending of an old system to be replaced by something new? In the case of the Glorious Revolution, it was quite the opposite. The Glorious Revolution was almost bloodless, and it was a revolution against change rather than for change. It all started with England's greatest fear: a Catholic monarch.

If you are interested in what James II was really like, you should read the profile on him in Chapter 3, but to understand why the Glorious Revolution occurred, there are a few key things to know.

1. James II was Roman Catholic. This made him instantly distrustful in the eyes of pretty much every proper English person.
2. James II reacted to the distrust of his people poorly. Feeling that he could not trust Anglicans, he began to fill his court full of Catholics and Dissenters, two unpopular groups.
3. James II made the mistake of trying to push more religious tolerance on the English people. He wanted to repeal the discriminatory laws against Catholics and Dissenters. While today, we can hopefully see that discrimination based on religion is bad, in 17th-century England, religious tolerance was a very unpopular move.
4. James II's final sin was being a father. While he had two Protestant daughters, in 1688, James's new Catholic wife gave birth to a son. The nation was appalled. A Catholic king was one thing, but a Catholic heir was unbearable.

Thanks to a combination of these four things, James II was a very unpopular king. In fact, he was so unpopular that in the summer his son was born, a group of England's most powerful men took a drastic step. They invited William of Orange to invade England.

But who was William of Orange? William of Orange was the husband of James's eldest daughter Mary. She was, thus, excluding James II's new son, next in line for the throne, and she was a good Protestant. What's more, her husband, William, was a capable military commander. He was deeply involved in a conflict with the Catholic nation of France, and he saw helping rid England of its Catholic monarch as a way to secure English help. He was the Protestant savior who would rescue England from the Catholics.

William of Orange landing in England by Hoynck van Papendrecht.
https://commons.wikimedia.org/wiki/File:William_of_Orange_III_and_his_Dutch_army_1_and_in_Brixham,_1688.jpg

On November 5th, 1688, William of Orange landed in England with an invading force. While landing had proven easy due to fortuitous winds, James II still had a large army. It was very likely that he would succeed in driving the would-be invader back into the sea.

At least, it should have been very likely, but this was an invader who had been invited by James II's own people, and those frayed loyalties soon began to show. James II's advisers and commanders abandoned him, defecting to William's side. James saw the writing on the wall and made his escape, fleeing to the continent.

After James II had made his escape, William of Orange marched into London at the head of an invading army that he hadn't even had to use. While there was a debate in Parliament over whether to give the crown to William, it was ultimately decided that in fleeing, James II had abdicated the throne. William and Mary were made the king and queen of England.

The Glorious Revolution got its name because it was a bloodless and extremely smooth transition of power. This smooth transition also caused people to think that it was divinely ordained, adding to the idea of it being "glorious."

The Glorious Revolution was proof that not every revolution had to be as bloody as the English Civil War. Ironically though, the Glorious Revolution was not too revolutionary. It was a revolution started over the fear of Catholicism and a distaste for religious tolerance.

Chapter 11: Societal Structure

So far in this book, we have spent the majority of our focus on the larger trends and events of the period. We have talked about revolutions, monarchs, religion, and trade. These are all the broad strokes that make up history.

But what about the small strokes of history? What was life like in England in the 16th and 17th centuries? What was the difference in the daily lives of the elite and the poor? In this chapter, we will take a look at early modern English society. From the hierarchical structure to the differences between genders and more, we will learn what one could expect out of life in early modern England.

The Great Chain of Being

The fact that society tends to break into different classes is a universal fact of humanity. When you put enough people together for a long enough period, eventually there emerges the "haves" and the "have nots." The fundamental economic problem of scarcity means that as long as we have limited resources, there will always be the rich and the poor.

However, while the existence of disparity in economics means that a class divide is almost inevitable, social classes are far from universal in how they appear in each society. The de facto divides of economics are often only the beginning. They become permanent or are added to by divides based on things like race, bloodlines, religion, etc. The picture of the "haves" and the "have nots" becomes far more complex when we add in these other social considerations. At its most basic, societal structures may be very similar across time and space, but the individual context makes that structure unique. So, our question then is not whether early modern England had social classes but what defined this period and made its social classes unique.

In early modern England, the governing principle that supported the social hierarchy was a philosophical concept known as the Great Chain of Being. The Great Chain of Being was first introduced by the Neoplatonists and saw a revival of interest in Europe during the Renaissance. It consists of three major points: plenitude, continuity, and gradation.

Plenitude is the idea that the universe is "full." Everything possible exists. Continuity is the idea that while the universe is infinitely diverse (as established in the point of plenitude), everything in the universe shares an attribute with something else. Nothing is totally unique. The final point, gradation, then says that the commonalities between the different components of the universe are not random but exist in a linear hierarchy. The top of this hierarchy is perfection itself, which was commonly understood to be God, and the hierarchy then goes down, with each component becoming less "perfect" until it covers everything in existence.

You may be wondering what such a philosophical concept has to do with social structure, and the answer lies in large part with the concept of hierarchy. The Great Chain of Being sees the universe as being ordered through a hierarchy. If the universe is a hierarchy, then the natural social hierarchy that emerges through economics and other factors is a part of the order of the universe. It is not just that a noble has more money and therefore is in a higher position than a yeoman. It is that this disparity is integral to the very nature of existence. The Great Chain of Being provides an explanation for and justification of social classes. To attempt to break out of one's social class would be to overturn the very order of the universe. To uphold stability, the social hierarchy must be maintained.

Before you immediately dismiss this understanding of the world as nothing more than a trick to keep the lower classes down, you should remember that people in this time were more afraid of anarchy. They were emerging from the Middle Ages, which was a time full of bloody internal conflicts. For the people of early modern England, especially the elite, it was more important to maintain order than it was to ensure that people had personal freedom. This is not to say they were correct about the Great Chain of Being, but we should remember that different values cause society to be structured differently. If a society values order more than freedom, it tends to be stricter about social hierarchies.

The Social Classes

So, what were the social classes in early modern England? Today, we might use terms like the upper, middle, and lower class, but in early modern England, things were a bit more specific. The social classes in order were the nobility, the gentry, the yeomanry, and the poor.

The nobility and the gentry were the elite of society. Nobles were those who held aristocratic titles. Besides royalty, the nobility includes (in order of rank) dukes, marquesses, earls, viscounts, and barons. These are the members of English society who sat in the House of Lords and who surrounded the monarch. The early modern period saw an increase in the number of noble families. After the bloody Wars of the Roses, the number of noble families left in England was less than fifty. That number steadily grew throughout the 16th and 17th centuries, but even so, the nobility made up a very small portion of society, with the total number of noble families in the early modern period reaching less than two hundred.

By contrast, the gentry grew much more rapidly, and part of the reason for that was that the understanding of who exactly qualified as a gentleman was expanding. Traditionally, gentlemen were those who owned land but were not part of the nobility. This included knights, esquires, and baronets, a title added by James I. Gentlemen could also include those without any title who owned an estate. This understanding of a gentleman began to expand once professionals with an education could be considered members of the gentry.

In short, the definition of a gentleman was a bit vague. The main thing for all of the elite was that they did not work. This did not mean that the nobility and gentry sat around doing nothing all the time (although that was part of it). The definition of work in those days meant manual labor. The elite did not work with their hands, but they did work in the government and ran their estates.

The next group on the social ladder was the yeomen, who were the closest to the middle class. Yeomen either owned land or were freeholders (people who technically rented land but who could not be evicted and who could do with the land what they wanted). Yeomen generally worked their own land but were well off enough to have farmhands and servants as well. Their sons (and daughters on occasion) often received at least some education.

These top three groups were the ones who owned all the land in England, but they only made up around 10 percent of the population. The other 90 percent of people in England were considered poor.

The poor class is a very broad term that encompasses a wide spectrum. Those just below the yeomen were cottagers and husbandmen. Husbandmen were tenants who rented land that they worked for food and income. The terms of their leases were often harsh, and they could be thrown out at any time. Cottagers rented cottages from landlords but typically had little to no land, leaving them to earn wages to support themselves.

After the husbandmen and cottagers were the homeless, those who migrated for work or who had become destitute to the point of losing their homes. Society had no place for these people. They did not fit into the established social order of landlords and tenants, thus violating the Great Chain of Being. Because of this violation of the natural order, this group was widely mistrusted, yet their numbers continued to grow.

There was a significant gap between husbandmen and the migratory poor without a home, but they were all included in a single social class because of how easy it was to move between them. Social classes back then had fairly rigid boundaries. It was not easy (or often even realistically possible) to move between social classes, but when hard times came, it was very easy for a cottager or husbandman to become completely impoverished and lose their homes.

The Growing Poor

Poverty and the growing number of migratory poor increased in early modern England.

The biggest reason for the increase in the number of poor was a simple matter of arithmetic. The population in early modern England was increasing drastically, more than doubling in seventy-five years (from 1525 to 1600).

Unfortunately, agricultural technology did not advance as rapidly. Food production did not increase at the same rate as the population. This caused food prices to increase while wages remained the same. The result was inevitable for many people. They could not buy food and pay their rent. Eventually, they lost their homes and had to resort to begging or wandering in search of work.

The increasing number of poor became an even bigger issue after the Reformation and dissolution of monasteries. Catholicism's emphasis on good works made taking care of the poor a duty. With the Protestant emphasis on faith alone, the amount of private charity gradually declined.

Worse than this was the dissolution of the monasteries. Monasteries had been places where the poor could seek medical attention and other basic needs. With them gone, England had lost its biggest charitable institutions at a time when poverty was on the rise.

Because of these issues, England's first Poor Law was passed during Elizabeth I's reign. For the first time, the poor were considered to be the responsibility of the state rather than the church. The new laws made each local parish responsible for caring for their poor, and the money for this was raised through local taxes.

How did the government help the poor, though? The able-bodied poor were sent to workhouses, where they performed some sort of work, such as spinning wool, and were, in theory, cared for in exchange. Workhouses were not nice places. Families were separated, and the inhabitants were often treated harshly.

The miserable state of workhouses demonstrates the overall hostile view many people in this era had of the poor. Able-bodied people who did not work were seen as lazy and criminals. There was little understanding of the idea that there might be more people than jobs. This had never been the case before, so society viewed this growing class of vagrants as purposefully deviant. Stories about groups of hardened criminal bands wandering the countryside abounded while being completely unfounded.

The mistrust and harsh treatment caused many of the poor to seek a better life somewhere else. Many chose to travel to the colonies as indentured servants. Some colonies were even designed to provide a place for England's growing number of debtors and other undesirables.

This poverty problem was one way in which we see England straining to grow. This period was the beginning of modernization, but that development did not come without challenges.

Private Life

Those are the groups that made up the societal structure in early modern England, but what was life like for the different classes? As you can probably guess, life was quite different for the elite than it was for the lower classes.

During the Middle Ages, the upper classes were the fighters of society. Feudalism was a system based on the idea that the lower classes worked the land and provided the necessities of life while the upper classes protected the land. In the early modern era, the ruling elite's role began to shift from focusing on warfare to service. The nobility were the administrators who ran the government and, through it, the economy, the justice system, and more.

These types of roles meant that upper-class life was a public affair. When noblewomen gave birth, their babies were typically handed over to a wet nurse so that the mother could return to running the household as quickly as possible. Marriage was an economic and strategic exchange that required planning and impacted far more than just the couple. As time went on, nobles started spending more time in London instead of at their secluded country estates, as they wanted to be close to the seat of government and the positions they either held or wanted. The medieval era had seen local lords exercising control over a particular region. The early modern era saw the power of the upper classes become more nationalized in the central government.

The increasing public role of the upper classes put a strain on their private lives. Married couples might spend most of their lives apart, as wives stayed in the country running the estates while their husbands worked in London. Children were separated from their parents almost as soon as they were born. Even when at home, the elite were expected to frequently act as hosts.

We can see the effect this had on the psyche of the upper classes in the layout of their homes. The homes of the wealthy tended to be in the shape of an E or an H, which allowed for distinct wings. One side of the house would be for public life, such as lavish dinners and greeting guests. The other side was the family's private chambers, where they could retreat from the public eye. This period even saw the inclusion of a withdrawing room (this term was eventually shortened to drawing room) where the family could relax in private.

So, being a part of the upper class was not all banquets and balls. There was a duty that came with it. You were expected to serve, and that meant that it was difficult to have a rich personal life. However, that does not mean that being wealthy was a burden. The elite still had it pretty easy. They prided themselves on never having to do manual labor and on being idle. They had a privileged position, even if it did come with a string or two.

In some ways, the experience of the lower classes was the exact opposite of that. While in the nobility, a husband and wife might spend most of the year living in separate parts of the country, spouses with less money and lower positions usually worked alongside each other. Children were nursed and raised by their actual mothers instead of by wet nurses and tutors. Family units also tended to be much smaller since homes were not big enough to house multiple generations. The lower life expectancy meant that multiple generations also rarely occurred.

Marriage was not nearly as business-like for the poor, but there were still economic considerations. A man had to be able to support his wife, and it often took years for a man to get to the point where he could do that. Because of this, the poor tended to marry far later in life than the rich, which also meant they often had fewer children because the women had fewer childbearing years left by the time they married.

So, the poor had more opportunities to choose their spouses, spend time with their children, and generally be with their families more, but it was still hard to be a poor person. Your economic position was insecure. A few years of bad harvests could turn a husbandman into a vagrant, or your landlord could kick you off his land without warning. Food prices were rising, wages were not increasing at the same rate, and the wool industry, which was England's biggest industry, stagnated in the late 16th and early 17th centuries. Early modern England was a place where the poor were getting poorer while the rich got richer, and the tensions this placed on society erupted in the form of riots and popular rebellions.

Still, a poor person in early modern England had it better than a poor person in the medieval era. The houses of even the poor were sturdier and larger. While food prices were a problem, access to food was less of one thanks to the expansion of trade. You were far less likely to sleep on a dirt floor or die of starvation. For these reasons, we must acknowledge that England was making progress. The social classes remained distinct, but what life was like at the bottom of the hierarchy was slowly improving.

Chapter 12: Battles and Wars Abroad

When examining the history of a particular country, there is a danger of developing tunnel vision. England was not isolated from the rest of the world at this time. In fact, it was interacting more than ever with other countries, and not all of those interactions were friendly.

The early modern era saw the rise of world powers. Empires were beginning, and countries were pushing to dominate. How England handled itself in these conflicts against foreign nations would determine if it could rise to the status of superpower.

The Conflict with Spain (1585–1604)

During the first half of the 16th century, England had a relatively good relationship with Spain. However, that began to change when Elizabeth I took the throne in 1558.

Philip II of Spain had been married to Elizabeth's half-sister, Queen Mary. When the Protestant Elizabeth took the throne, there was apprehension about whether Philip II would make a move to push England back to Catholicism. Although nothing happened at the time, and Philip appeared to have no problem with his sister-in-law taking the throne, it was the beginning of a mistrustful relationship that would eventually explode into open hostilities.

Surprisingly, religion did not ultimately cause the split between Spain and England. It was Spain's success. During the first half of Elizabeth I's reign, Spain's empire continued to grow and, with it, its wealth and power. England grew increasingly uncomfortable with the might of this Catholic kingdom and increasingly desirous of a piece of what Spain had.

When the Spanish attacked an English slave fleet in 1568, Elizabeth I had the excuse she needed to start taking a bite out of Spain. English privateers soon began raiding Spanish settlements and ships, stealing both goods and bullion. Elizabeth I officially denounced these acts, but unofficially, she authorized and even encouraged them. But Spain had a way to indirectly fire back at England.

Elizabeth I was unmarried and thus without an heir. Her closest royal relative was Mary, Queen of Scots. Mary had been kicked out of Scotland and was currently residing in England. She had one quality that made her useful to the Spanish. Mary, Queen of Scots was Roman Catholic.

There were still many Roman Catholics in England who found the idea of a Roman Catholic on the throne appealing. Thus, Mary, Queen of Scots was the center of plots and conspiracies, and it is almost certain that the Spanish were involved in a number of these. A Roman Catholic would be far more sympathetic to the Spanish than the piracy-approving Protestant Queen Elizabeth I.

Piracy and plots caused tensions between Spain and England to rise, but the two countries might have managed to keep the peace were it not for another problem: the Netherlands. The Netherlands had become a Spanish possession in 1556 when Philip II inherited the crown, and the Dutch were not thrilled about it. In the late 1560s, a revolt against Spanish rule broke out in the north of the Netherlands, which was a Calvinist-dominated area that was unhappy with the rule of Catholic Spain.

Elizabeth I had to make a decision. Would she support her fellow monarch Philip II, or would she support the Dutch Protestants? While Elizabeth I was notorious for delaying such momentous decisions, her hand was forced by circumstances. A Spanish ship carrying quite a lot of gold was forced to shelter in an

English port. The Spanish assumed the English would seize the ship and arrested English merchants in the Netherlands, seizing these English goods in retaliation for something Elizabeth I had not done yet. Her response was to do exactly what they expected. She seized the Spanish ship and began supporting the Dutch rebels with money.

England and Spain had once been allies, but by 1568, the trust between them had completely disappeared. Still, neither country was eager for war, and it would take another seventeen years for open hostilities to erupt. In 1585, Elizabeth I sent English troops to the Netherlands to support the rebellion. For Philip II, it was an act of war. The Spanish king soon began making plans to invade England.

Philip II had every intention of thoroughly crushing the English. Over the next 3 years, he amassed an invasion fleet of 130 ships. The fleet was to carry over thirty thousand troops for a full-scale invasion of England.

Elizabeth I did not have an army that could hope to compete with such a force. The English army was made up of poorly trained or completely untrained troops. Spain's army was well trained and well paid. If the Spanish landed their army, England would be in trouble. Their only real chance was to stop the fleet at sea.

England's Royal Navy was not in as terrible of a position as you might think. The Spanish fleet was large, but it was also slower and lacked a significant number of heavy cannons, which would have allowed them to engage the English at a distance.

As the Spanish fleet proceeded through the Channel, it was harried by the more maneuverable English ships. When the fleet docked at Calais, the English sent fire ships into the harbor, forcing the fleet to scatter. Once they were out of formation, they were easy targets for the Royal Navy.

Hopes of invasion were now over. The Spanish fleet retreated, but the ships were unable to make the passage through the Channel because it was controlled by the English. Instead, they sailed around Scotland and Ireland, but unfavorable winds kept the ships floundering. By the time the armada limped back to Spain, half of it was gone.

The *Defeat of the Spanish Armada* by Philip James de Loutherbourg.
https://commons.wikimedia.org/wiki/File:Defeat_of_the_Spanish_Armada,_8_August_1588_RMG_BHC0264.tiff

The defeat of the Spanish Armada was a major moment for England. They had proven themselves able to stand against Europe's mightiest power, which did a lot for English confidence. England's command of the seas would go on to be a major reason for why it was able to dominate the empire game in the coming centuries.

While the defeat of the Spanish Armada in 1588 was a triumph for England, it was not the end of the conflict with Spain. The two superpowers continued to clash. England continued to support the Dutch rebels, and English privateers raided Spanish settlements in the New World with waning success. Spain, in turn, supported an Irish rebellion against England that turned into a very costly war.

The conflict with Spain was never declared war, but the expense of being in constant open hostilities with another nation put a strain on the English government. Parliament gained more power since Queen Elizabeth I needed more and more funds for military expeditions. This planted the seeds of the dispute between Parliament and the monarch, which would lead to the English Civil

War decades later.

The Anglo-Dutch Wars

Spain was not the only country that England found itself competing with for command of the seas and trade. The Netherlands was also one of England's main rivals. England fought three wars against the Dutch between 1652 and 1672.

England's wars with the Dutch were mostly naval, as the two countries vied for control of the seas. The First Anglo-Dutch War erupted in 1652 due to high tensions over the control of trade. The English were dominant in this first conflict, and hostilities ended in 1654.

In the Second Anglo-Dutch War, the English were not as successful. The war began in 1665. In the same year, a plague epidemic broke out, and the following year, the Great Fire of London raged. By 1667, Charles II's government was broke, strained, and eager to win the war, but the Dutch wanted to press their advantage.

In 1667, the Dutch raided the dockyards in the Medway. The ships docked there had only skeleton crews, making them essentially defenseless. The Dutch were able to capture and burn several ships and even sailed off with the ship named *Royal Charles*. It was a great embarrassment to the English. They had been completely unable to defend themselves. Peace was made shortly after this.

After the embarrassment of the Raid on the Medway, England was eager to take revenge on the Dutch. War again broke out in 1672 but this time as part of a larger European conflict. In this war, England allied with France against the Netherlands. The Netherlands was able to hold off invasion attempts for two years. England dropped out of the alliance, making peace with the Netherlands in 1674. Soon after this, the Glorious Revolution saw the two countries sharing a ruler for a time. With a shared ruler came shared goals, namely stopping the French, and there would be around a century of peace between the Netherlands and England.

The conflict between the Netherlands and England demonstrates how economic rivalries led to bloodshed in this period. Both countries wanted to control trade, and they were willing to fight each other for that control.

War of the Grand Alliance (1688–1697)

When William of Orange invaded England in 1688 and became William III of England, it was largely with one goal in mind. He wanted England's aid in putting a halt to France's expansion efforts.

To William of Orange, France was a growing tyrant that was conquering Protestant Europe. France was making moves to absorb both the Dutch and the Spanish into its empire. Stopping France's expansion was William III's goal in life, and while he saw the English as being central to that goal, the English did not necessarily agree. They were part of a small country separated from the continent by the Channel. They did not see themselves as a superpower, and they did not see William's war against the French as affecting them. After fighting both the Spanish and the Dutch themselves in the last century, it would be a hard sell to convince the English that they should commit to an expensive war on the continent.

However, whether they meant to or not, the English had already committed themselves to a side in the conflict. They had invited William of Orange to depose James II. After the Glorious Revolution, France supported James II in his hopes of reclaiming the throne, supporting him directly when he landed in Ireland in the hopes of winning his kingdom back. If England was against James II, then they were against France.

So, in choosing William III over James II, England found that it had agreed to an alliance against France. Although the English never showed great enthusiasm for the war, they were a part of the Grand Alliance, which included England, the United Provinces of the Netherlands, Austria, Spain, and other smaller states.

For a war that lasted nine years, the War of the Grand Alliance achieved relatively little. The war was mostly a matter of long sieges and stalemates. Neither side could win a decisive victory, and in

1697, peace was established by the Treaty of Rijswijk. The only problem was that the treaty did not fix anything. France still had hopes of expanding its empire, and the rest of Europe still did not want that to happen. The same issues would turn into another war only four years later.

The War of the Spanish Succession (1701–1714)

The War of the Spanish Succession was a continuation of the problems from the War of the Grand Alliance. The general issue was France's expansionist drive, but the specific problem was the Spanish succession.

Charles II was the childless king of Spain and the last of the Spanish Habsburgs. When he died, there would be no male heir to take the Spanish throne. Thanks to the constant marriage alliances of European royalty, both the Bourbon dynasty of France and the Austrian branch of the Habsburgs had fairly equal claims to the Spanish throne.

As Charles II's death drew closer, it became clearer that war was inevitable. Attempts were made to create a treaty that would divide the Spanish Empire rather than allow one person to inherit the entire thing, but no solution could be found that was satisfactory to everyone. The Spanish Empire was vast, and neither the Habsburgs nor the Bourbons were willing to give it up without a fight. Charles II died in 1700. King Louis XIV of France named his grandson, Philip, king of Spain, and war soon followed.

Technically, this had nothing to do with England directly, and England might have stayed out of the fight had Louis XIV not acknowledged James II's son as James III, the rightful king of England. If France was going to ally itself with England's enemies, then France could not be allowed to gain the Spanish Empire's power and wealth.

The military history of this thirteen-year war is complex. There were multiple fronts, many countries involved, and different stages to the conflict. There were several attempts at peace negotiations, but the war continued to drag on and on. England and its allies had many successes, thanks in large part to the military mind of John Churchill, but they could never gain enough ground or win a victory that would devastate France into ending the war.

In some ways, the war was simply too big. It covered too much ground for one side to seize complete control, and the military strategies of the time would not commit enough men to a bold offensive maneuver that would end the war in one stroke. The only way the war was going to end was through negotiations.

By 1711, Queen Anne and the majority of Parliament had had enough of the war, despite John Churchill's victories. The war was expensive, and those victories were not getting them closer to completely overwhelming France and forcing a surrender. It would take over two years to finalize the agreement that became the Treaty of Utrecht.

The Treaty of Utrecht was a true master play for Britain, although, on the surface, it did not appear that way to Britain's allies. Britain acknowledged Philip V as the king of Spain, which was the issue that had started the war in the first place, but France had to promise that Philip and his descendants were exempt from the French line of succession. The Crowns of France and Spain could never be united.

Britain also gained territories in the treaty, such as Gibraltar, Minorca, Nova Scotia, Newfoundland, Hudson's Bay, and St. Kitts. Another part of the treaty was the Asiento, which gave British slave traders a thirty-year monopoly on selling slaves to the Spanish Empire. King Louis XIV also had to promise to stop supporting James III's aims on the English crown.

For many, the territories Britain gained in the treaty and the promises the treaty required of France were nowhere near enough after thirteen years' worth of blood and money poured into the war. However, the Treaty of Utrecht placed Britain in a position that would allow it to become the dominant world power over the next century.

The territories Britain gained allowed it to expand its trading empire, and the Asiento was a further boon to Britain's trading power. Britain was setting itself up to prosper, while France had been broken economically by the war. Including the War of the Grand Alliance, France had been fighting for over twenty years. The country was spent, so while the Treaty of Utrecht might not have been harsh enough on France for some, there was no need for it to be. While France tried to recover from its scheme of making a grand empire, Britain continued to amass more wealth from its new colonies and trading deals.

This wealth would place Britain in a superior position as it continued to clash with France over the next century, allowing it to come out on top the vast majority of the time. The War of the Spanish Succession initially had very little to do with England, but thanks to its involvement in the war and the gains made in the Treaty of Utrecht, England was able to position itself to dominate and become the world's largest empire.

Chapter 13: Scotland and Wales

Although they share an island and are now part of the same nation, for most of their history, England, Wales, and Scotland have been three distinct countries.

The union of the island began in the medieval era with Edward I. Edward I conquered Wales in the 13th century. He nearly conquered Scotland as well, but the Scottish were able to maintain their sovereignty after a long conflict. From this point on, the heir of the English throne was given the title Prince of Wales as a sign of England's control over this territory.

However, Wales was not politically united with England at this time. While English kings ruled Wales by right of conquest, their governments remained separate. The justice system was different, and the Welsh had no members in the English Parliament. It was only in the early modern era that Wales officially joined England. Under Henry VIII, the Act of Union, which was passed in 1536, united Wales and England. English law would be used in Welsh courts, and Wales was divided up into local districts (shires and boroughs), which meant they could now elect members to English Parliament. Essentially, Wales and England were both operating under the same rule book, whereas before, they had the same king but different laws.

Scotland's union with England would eventually follow a similar pattern. When Elizabeth I died in 1604, her closest heir was James VI of Scotland. From that point on, England and Scotland had the same monarch. However, the two countries were not officially united until about one hundred years later with the 1707 Acts of Union during Queen Anne's reign. This act created the country of Great Britain.

Union Jack. (Source: Original code by Stefan-Xp with modifications to ratio by Yaddah., *https://commons.wikimedia.org/wiki/File:Flag_of_the_United_Kingdom_(3-5).svg*

Of course, the history of England, Scotland, and Wales in the early modern period involves a lot more than acts of union. While these three places made up the country of Great Britain, they were (and still are) three distinct places with complex and changing relationships. Here's a bit of what those relationships were like during the early modern period.

Scotland in the Tudor Era

Relations between England and Scotland had always been, for lack of a better word, tense. England repeatedly tried to conquer Scotland in the Middle Ages, and the northern country repeatedly tried to make life difficult for the English. Scottish raids over the Anglo-Scottish border were common, and one of Scotland's biggest allies was also one of England's biggest enemies: France. France and Scotland had been allies for so long that the relationship had come to be known as simply the Auld Alliance.

So, at the start of the early modern era, Scotland and England were not exactly best friends, and having an enemy as your nearest neighbor is enough to make anyone nervous. It is no wonder that the first Tudor king, Henry VII, married his daughter Margaret to James IV of Scotland in 1503. This marriage secured peace for a time, but by 1513, Scotland and England were at blows again when Henry VIII invaded France, triggering Scotland to respond due to the Auld Alliance.

As the 16th century wore on, however, Scotland soon found itself infected by the same disease that was infecting all of Europe: the Reformation. Unlike England, which experienced a top-down Reformation, Scotland's monarchs remained Catholic for much longer. Scotland also had a weaker central government that exercised less control over the country. Scottish nobles wielded considerable political power, and as the Reformation spread throughout Scotland, many of these nobles (called lairds in Scotland), particularly those in the Lowlands, turned to Protestantism.

This was partially due to the preaching of men like John Knox, but it also was because of an increasing Scottish desire to break away from French influence. The last Scottish king, James V, died in 1542, leaving an infant daughter as queen and Scotland in the hands of her mother, Mary of Guise, who acted as regent. Mary of Guise was French and Catholic, and many Scottish lairds thought that she was turning Scotland into a French auxiliary. These suspicions were only exacerbated by Mary sending her daughter, who was technically the queen of Scotland, to be raised and educated in France. Mary of Guise also arranged for her daughter to marry the future French king, Francis II, making James V's daughter the queen of France and Scotland. With these acts, Mary of Guise was clearly tying Scotland more closely to the French, and embracing the new religion was a way to buck against the French and declare Scottish autonomy.

This bucking turned into a full rebellion in 1559, and the French sent troops to help Mary of Guise seize control again. The Scottish rebels then turned to England and Elizabeth I for assistance. This put Elizabeth I in a dilemma. She could support the Protestant rebels, declaring her sympathy with Protestantism, or she could support Mary of Guise, showing her support for a fellow monarch. It was always a risky suggestion for one monarch to help those rebelling against the authority of another monarch.

Ultimately, though, this was an opportunity for England to break up the Auld Alliance. If the French succeeded in putting Mary of Guise back in control of Scotland, England would have a Catholic enemy on its northern border, and what's worse, a Catholic enemy whose monarch (Mary, Queen of Scots) was also Elizabeth's cousin and the next in line for the English throne. England sided with the Scottish rebels. The conflict ended shortly after it began, thanks to the death of Mary of Guise in 1560. The Treaty of Edinburgh, which officially ended the hostilities, established religious tolerance in Scotland and set up a ruling council that was half Protestant and half Catholic.

Elizabeth I's decision to support the rebels proved to be a good move for England. Tensions between the two countries lessened considerably after this, and there was peace on the Anglo-Scottish border. The two countries were destined to grow even closer when the Scottish king became the next English monarch.

Same Monarch, Different Kingdoms

In 1603, James VI of Scotland became James I of England. We have talked in greater detail about how this came, so now let's look at what having the same monarch did to the relations between Scotland and England.

If you are thinking that one king trying to rule two different kingdoms with different governments and laws sounds like a bad idea, you wouldn't be the only one. James I thought the same thing, and when he first took the crown of England, he did his best to remedy the situation by promoting a union. Unfortunately for James I, England was having none of it. The English Parliament resolutely rejected the idea of a union with Scotland, revealing their deeply held prejudices. The English viewed their northern neighbors as poor and backward. They felt that to unite with Scotland would be to take on a burden.

So, where did this leave Scotland? Their king had headed off to London, where the Stuart monarchs would remain, ruling Scotland from afar. A king could not keep in touch with his people over such a long distance, and this became glaringly evident when Charles I tried to impose the English *Book of Common Prayer* on the Presbyterian Scots.

One should never underestimate what people are willing to do for their religious convictions. The Scottish didn't just riot or protest. In 1638, the Scottish created a document entitled the New Covenant, which was essentially a new constitution organizing the church and state. Rearranging the government without the king's consent can only be seen as an open rebellion. The Scottish rebels were known as the Covenanters after the document they had created. Charles I had to get Scotland in line. This was the start of the First Bishops' War.

The First Bishops' War didn't last very long. Charles I found that his English army was unenthusiastic about his cause, and he was broke. A truce was established in 1639, but it was only temporary. In England, things were falling apart. Charles I hadn't called Parliament to meet in eleven years, but he desperately needed funds to face the Scottish rebellion. The Scots pushed their advantage, starting the Second Bishops' War in 1640. They were quickly able to invade the north of England, forcing Charles I to turn to the English Parliament for assistance. This was the parliament that would come to be known as the Long Parliament and led to the English Civil War.

So, to some degree, the Scots caused the English Civil War, and their involvement in the conflict did not stop there. The English Civil War is perhaps more accurately called the War of the Three Kingdoms. Charles I was king of Scotland, England, and Ireland, so the war against him came to involve all three nations.

At first, Scotland was against Charles I. After all, it had technically been the first to rebel, but after Charles I was captured and the unfruitful negotiations began, Scotland entered its own negotiations with Charles I and agreed to restore him. This led to the outbreak of the Second English Civil War, but Oliver Cromwell's armies were able to stop the Scottish with ease. Charles I was soon executed, and Scotland found itself without a king for the next eleven years.

While the two countries were still politically separate entities, having the same king meant that Scotland found itself dragged along by what was happening in England, often whether it wanted to or not. This was again the case after the Glorious Revolution deposed James II. Jacobitism, which was the belief that James II and his male heirs were the rightful rulers of England, Scotland, and Ireland, had the strongest following in Scotland.

How is that possible though? Weren't the Scots Presbyterians? Why would they support a Catholic king? The history of Scotland during this period deserves an entire book of its own, but in short, things were more complex than just the idea that Scotland was full of Presbyterians after the Reformation. Before the Glorious Revolution, Scotland had seen a revival of Catholic power and persecution of Presbyterians. When the Glorious Revolution occurred, it returned the Presbyterians to power, but they returned to power full of resentment for the previous decade of bad treatment. The result was a less glorious and more bloody revolution in Scotland.

This bad blood only served to isolate certain groups: Episcopalians in the Lowlands and Catholics in the Highlands. These two groups would form the core of the staunch Jacobite movement that developed in Scotland over the next several decades.

With events like the English Civil War (the War of the Three Kingdoms) and the Glorious Revolution, it was obvious that Scotland and England were irretrievably intertwined, but it was unclear if that would continue. The Scottish were becoming increasingly annoyed at being ruled by London. In the early 18th century, the Scottish Parliament began passing laws that were anti-English, including one that said that after Queen Anne's death, Scotland would choose its next monarch.

This was very alarming to the English. It was likely that Scotland would pick Prince James, the son of James II. This would put a Catholic pro-French monarch on England's northern border. It would be a return to the Auld Alliance and most likely a return to the constant feuding that had shaped most of Scotland's and England's history.

When James I tried to unite England and Scotland in 1603, the English had been opposed to the idea, but now they had the motivation to make the union happen. The only question was how they could convince the Scots, who were currently very unhappy with their southern neighbors.

In the end, it came down to economics. Scotland was a poor nation, and a union with England offered wealth. As part of the union agreement, Scotland would be able to trade freely with England and its colonies. England was a trading giant, and Scotland would become part of that system. If that was not convincing enough for the Scots, the English also paid them a lump sum called the Equivalent. This was out-and-out bribery, but it got the job done. The Scottish Parliament voted to end their own government.

Scotland was now part of England. It still retained its individuality in things like its church and laws, but there was no parliament in Edinburgh. The Scots sat in the Parliament in London. Great Britain was born.

Wales: Same Kingdom, Different Language

Welsh flag.
https://commons.wikimedia.org/wiki/File:Flag_of_Wales.svg

We have examined England's relationship with its northern neighbor, but what about its western neighbor? As we mentioned in the introduction to this chapter, England conquered Wales back in the 13th century, but it was not until Henry VIII's reign that the two were officially united.

Why did Henry VIII suddenly decide to officially make Wales part of England? Was there some sort of pressure like with Scottish unification?

Not really. Unification with Wales was largely because Henry VIII realized that it would make governing a lot easier. As we mentioned in Chapter 1, the Tudor era saw the strengthening and centralization of the national government. To effectively rule his entire realm from London, Henry VIII needed Wales to use the same judicial system and districts. It was unification for the sake of bureaucracy.

But unification did not mean total assimilation. Wales remained its own place with its own culture, and we can see this best in its language. Although Wales had been conquered by England for over three centuries, in the early modern era, Welsh remained the main language. Most Welsh people did not know English.

The language difference was so pronounced that part of the unification treaty stipulated that all Welshmen who held government positions had to be able to speak English. This created a situation in which the Welsh elite were bilingual. The majority of people still only knew Welsh and had to rely on the bilingual elite for information from England.

The dominance of Welsh created an interesting situation in Wales with the arrival of the Reformation. The Reformation emphasized the importance of scripture, and as part of this, the Bible was translated into English so that the average person could read it. After the Reformation, church services were conducted in English instead of Latin. However, for the average person in Wales, religious services in English were little better than religious services in Latin.

Some leading Welsh scholars became convinced that Welsh translations of the Bible were necessary, both for the sake of religion and the Welsh culture. They succeeded in getting Parliament to pass an act requiring the Bible to be translated into Welsh. The New Testament and the *Book of Common Prayer* were translated by 1567, and by 1588, the entire Bible had been translated into Welsh.

The translation of the Bible into Welsh was a huge achievement for the Welsh people and also a smart move politically for England. The translation of the Bible into Welsh connected the Protestant movement with Welsh culture. Instead of forcing an English Reformation down the throats of the Welsh, it became the Welsh Reformation. In other places in the British Isles where a different language was spoken, namely Ireland and the Scottish Highlands, the Bible was translated much later. Catholicism had a much stronger grip on these areas.

Wales was far more closely aligned with England than Scotland, but it was still a distinct place. Another time where we see this is in the English Civil War. There was much royalist support in Wales in the dispute between Charles I and Parliament, but in the end, it didn't do Charles I much good. Like Scotland, Wales was poorer and less populated than England. They were not in a position to threaten its larger and wealthier neighbor.

It would be some time before Wales began to catch up to England in terms of wealth. In the early modern era, Wales remained an agricultural society. Progress was essentially a matter of enclosing and cultivating more land so that less was wasted. The rich were getting richer since they gained control of even more land, and the poor only continued to get poorer.

Eventually, the economy of Wales would change with the discovery of coal and its importance to the Industrial Revolution, but in the early modern era, Wales remained an agricultural-based society.

Overall, Wales experienced far less tension with England than Scotland did at this time, which makes sense considering that Scotland was still a separate country until 1707. Still, it is a mistake to lump Wales and England together too much. Even in the 16th century, the Welsh were proud enough of their cultural differences to want the Bible in their language. Wales was politically and governmentally united with England while maintaining a distinct culture that has carried on to this day.

While non-Britons may confuse the three regions of Great Britain, Wales, England, and Scotland are united but unique. The early modern era was when the union known as Great Britain started, and it is a union that has lasted to this day.

Chapter 14: The Irish Question

Scotland, Wales, and England don't have this small region of the world entirely to themselves. There was a fourth kingdom in the British Isles, and its relationship with England was messy.

Ireland, like Wales, was initially conquered by England in the Middle Ages during the time of Henry II, but unlike Wales, English control of Ireland was far from total. The English only managed to subdue part of Ireland. In the area controlled by the English, which came to be called the Pale, the Anglo-Irish nobles held power. Outside of the Pale, Ireland was controlled by the Gaelic Irish, and the land was split among various sects and chieftains.

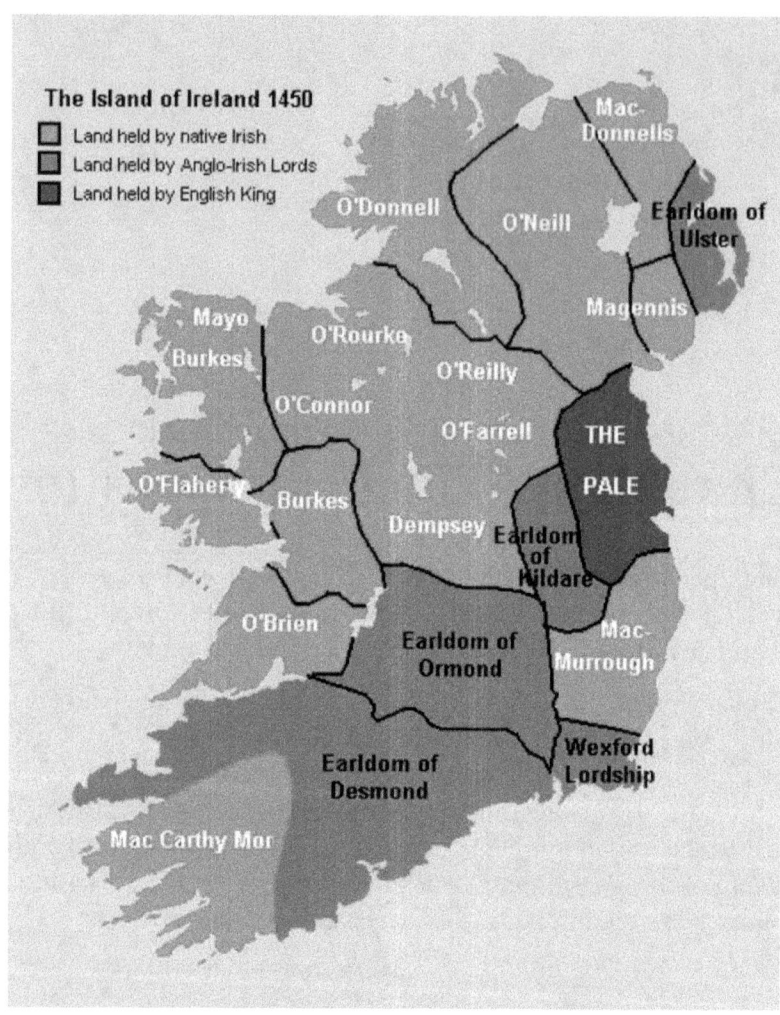

Ireland in 1450.
https://commons.wikimedia.org/wiki/File:Ireland_1450.png

But who exactly were the Anglo-Irish and the Gaelic Irish? The Gaelic Irish were the Gaelic-speaking Irish who had inhabited the island before Henry II's invasion. The Anglo-Irish were the English settlers who settled in Ireland after England conquered it in the Middle Ages. Over time, the Anglo-Irish came to accept many Gaelic customs and intermarried with the Gaelic Irish until they were far more Irish than English.

Ireland and the Early Tudors

This was the general situation when the Tudors took the throne. The Pale was under English control, but the majority of the island was controlled by the Gaelic Irish. Even within the Pale, the Anglo-Irish lords were often unruly, and their loyalty to the English Crown was questionable.

In fact, at the start of the Tudor era, Irish influence was particularly strong since there was a resurgence of Irish culture and influence around this time. The Irish Renaissance was heavily focused on poetry, and many Irish lords showed their power and sophistication by becoming patrons of these poets. The English rightly saw these poets as problematic because they encouraged a growing sense of Irish nationalism. The Tudors would soon find that maintaining control of Ireland would be problematic.

When Henry VII became the first Tudor monarch, Ireland was practically ruled by Gerald FitzGerald, Earl of Kildare. Kildare was an Irishman, and he maintained his power through alliances with both the Gaelic Irish and Anglo-Irish. Kildare was not especially loyal to the Tudor monarchy, so Henry VII replaced him, naming an Englishman, Edward Poynings, as the new lord deputy of Ireland.

Poynings discovered what almost every Englishman trying to control Ireland did. It was very expensive. Although Poynings was able to seize control and even passed several laws in an attempt to solidify English control, including the famous Poynings' Law, which subjected the Irish Parliament to the English monarch's control, his government was too expensive for Henry VII's taste. Henry VII withdrew Poynings and restored Kildare to control Ireland. Thanks to Kildare's complex series of alliances, he was the only man able to maintain effective control in Ireland.

When Kildare died, Henry VIII appointed his son to take his place as deputy. While such a move made sense to the English king, it demonstrated a misunderstanding of Irish politics. The Irish did not necessarily pass powerful positions from father to son, which means the younger Kildare did not gain immediate respect from the Irish simply because of his birth. The elder Kildare also ruled effectively because he understood the various allegiances and feuds that made up the Irish political landscape. His son had been raised in England and had none of this essential firsthand knowledge.

Thus, things in Ireland did not go as smoothly as Henry VIII expected. English control gradually slipped during the first half of Henry VIII's reign. The Gaelic lords simply felt no allegiance or fear of the English Crown outside the Pale, and even within it, the Anglo-Irish were too fond of their autonomy to be easily led. Relations between England and Ireland would only worsen with the Reformation.

Ireland and the Reformation

Throughout Europe, the Protestant Reformation proved the same thing over and over. The ruler of a nation and its people could not be of different religions. Either the people would force the ruler to change or leave, or the ruler would impose their will on the people. England saw how true this was from both directions when Henry VIII brought the Reformation to England due to his political goals and when the English people forced James II to leave for being Catholic. Presbyterian Scotland had rebelled against the Catholic Mary of Guise. A nation could not thrive if its rulers and people were of different religions.

Ireland was the only European country to learn this truth the long way. When Henry VIII broke with Rome and started the process that would turn England Protestant, the Reformation was inevitably going to make its way to the shores of Ireland. In 1536, another Act of Supremacy made Henry the head of the Irish Church, and in 1541, Henry VIII took the title "King of Ireland" (before this, English kings had simply been the "Lord of Ireland").

Henry VIII was on a mission to consolidate his control over Ireland, and as part of this mission, he began the "surrender and regrant" method. This was a policy where the Irish surrendered their lands only to have them regranted along with titles by the English Crown. While no specific mentions were made of religion in this policy, to surrender and accept titles from the English king, who had made himself head of the Irish Church, had clear implications. It would be an acceptance of England's authority and an acceptance of the Anglican Church. The Irish Catholics were not having it, and Protestantism made virtually no headway in Ireland. Practically all of the Gaelic Irish and most of the Anglo-Irish remained Catholic.

It's unclear why the Reformation completely failed in Ireland. Henry VIII likely expected some support from at least the Anglo-Irish within the Pale, but the Reformation only pushed this group closer to the Gaelic Irish and further from England. Some have speculated that if the Bible and the *Book of Common Prayer* had been translated into Gaelic, it would have had a greater impact on the religious sentiments of the Irish, much as the Welsh translation aided the Reformation in Wales. As it was, to the Irish, the Reformation was an English movement designed to grant the English king greater control over them.

Because of the stiff Irish resistance to the Reformation, little changed in Ireland during the reigns of Edward VI and Mary. The Reformation had made little to no progress to begin with, so Ireland did not experience the religious whiplash that England did under these monarchs. The rule of Elizabeth I, however, would not be as uneventful.

Elizabeth I and Irish Rebellions

Elizabeth I is a monarch often known for her political tact and skill, but little can be said that is positive about her policy regarding Ireland. After both her father and two half-siblings had gotten nowhere with the Irish, Elizabeth I seemed strangely determined to bring them in line.

Compared to Edward VI and Mary, Elizabeth's religious settlement was moderate. It was designed to please as many people as possible and keep the peace, but it was still not acceptable to the Irish. They remained strictly Catholic, and there were frequent rebellions against English rule and Protestantism. Unable to convert the Irish, Elizabeth I turned to a different method for subduing the island: plantations.

Plantations were lands taken from the Irish (usually Catholics) and redistributed to English settlers, who were Protestant. This usually occurred after a rebellion, such as after the Shane O'Neill

Rebellion and the Desmond Rebellion. England confiscated the rebels' lands and then redistributed them to loyal English subjects. It was a crude method of peace-making that relied on replacing the rebellious Irish population with a more obedient English one. This Protestant English population was known as the New English.

However, this method of replacing the rebellious population with a loyal population was not thorough enough to really work. The populations of the plantations were not as purely New English as they needed to be for England to truly dominate. The Anglo-Irish (also called the Old English) and the Gaelic Irish remained in large numbers, and they were still Catholic and opposed to English rule. Perhaps the worst of these rebellions was Tyrone Rebellion, also known as the Nine Years' War, which lasted from 1594 to 1603.

The Tyrone Rebellion took place in Ulster, the northernmost region of Ireland. Thanks to the plantations, Ulster was the only region of Ireland not heavily infected by the English. The earl of Tyrone, Hugh O'Neill, was the most powerful man in this region. It is unclear what precisely sparked the rebellion. O'Neill likely felt isolated and threatened by increasing English power and decided to strike first in 1594.

Going up against the far more organized and wealthy English was a risky move for O'Neill, but he did have a good sense of timing with his rebellion. The English were embroiled in other conflicts on the continent, which made it difficult for them to spare the resources to deal with the Irish rebellion. Furthermore, Spain, as a Catholic country and England's enemy, was willing to lend its support to O'Neill, though, in the end, this amounted to more moral support than the actual troops O'Neill needed.

The Tyrone Rebellion dragged on for nine years. At first, the English lacked the manpower to respond at all, but when English settlers began to be slaughtered, Elizabeth I had to respond. The first military commander she sent over was the earl of Essex, and he proved to be utterly incompetent. He was replaced in 1600 by Lord Mountjoy, who managed to force O'Neill to surrender in 1603.

The Tyrone Rebellion was a bitter and bloody war that only served to further sour Anglo-Irish relations. The warfare involved lots of guerrilla tactics, causing the deaths of many civilians and the destruction of much land and property, especially in Ulster but also in the southern regions of Ireland as well. The English showed no mercy in subduing the region, and while they were successful in the short term, this only deepened the Irish people's resentment of English rule.

Shortly after the Tyrone Rebellion, in 1607, many of the Irish nobility fled to Europe. Their goal was to garner Catholic support for their cause and return to reclaim their lands and power. However, they never returned. This event, known as the Flight of the Earls, left the Irish laypeople to be subjected to the whims of the English. The English government confiscated the lands of the earls who had fled and redistributed them to the New English settlers (including many Scots).

With these new settlements, Ulster suddenly had a large population of both English Protestants and Scottish Presbyterians, which has remained to the present day. This was the origin of what is now Northern Ireland, the only part of Ireland that is united with England in the United Kingdom.

New Dynasty, More Rebellions

After their experience under Elizabeth I, the Irish were relieved when James I took the throne, but their joy was short-lived. The new king made it clear almost immediately that he did not intend to relieve the persecution of Catholics, and he continued the expansion of the plantations, settling Ireland with English Protestants. These Protestants became the landlords, and the Irish, who used to own the lands, were either forced to move to infertile and hostile areas or become tenants, paying outrageous prices and being exploited.

So, once again, the Irish rebelled. Similar to the Tyrone Rebellion, they again waited for the perfect opportunity. It was the autumn of 1641. Charles I had been forced to call Parliament to deal with the Scottish rebellion in the north, and England was fracturing along Royalist and Parliamentary lines. The king was in an extremely weak position, which would hopefully make him willing to concede to demands. The time was ripe, and the Catholics of Ulster rose.

The uprising spread throughout the island, and after decades of building resentment, it quickly became bloody. While the stories of slaughter were likely exaggerated by the time they reached England, the Gaelic Irish did kill the New English settlers by the thousands. Despite this bloodshed, the Old English joined the Gaelic Irish in the rebellion in 1642, forming the Confederation of Kilkenny as a provisional government. The ties of religion had proved stronger than the ties of ancestry.

The Irish rebellion thoroughly frightened the English people. They were convinced that the evil Catholics were going to invade and kill all the Protestants. England needed to respond, but to do so, it needed to raise another army. It was at this point that Charles I and Parliament began taking separate military actions, and the English Civil War began. The Irish rebellion was the final push that forced the king and Parliament into warfare.

What happened to the Irish rebellion since the king and Parliament had turned on each other? For the next seven years, England was too busy with its own situation to send an army to pacify Ireland. The Irish were involved in the English Civil War during this time, siding with the king in the hopes of negotiating religious tolerance for Catholics (something the Puritan-led Parliament was not likely to grant).

But then, in 1649, Charles I was executed, and the new English Commonwealth turned its attention to Ireland. Cromwell and his army arrived within the year and proceeded to win back the island in a brutal fashion. The memory of the 1641 rebellion and slaughter of English settlers was still fresh. The English army killed Catholic priests and civilians. The soldiers burned and destroyed almost everything they came across. The destruction was so bad that over 200,000 died either directly through violence or by starvation.

After the island was officially reconquered, the English government returned to the plantation method, again confiscating land from Catholics and redistributing it to English Protestants. Persecution of Catholics in this period (when Puritans controlled the English government) reached a new high. So much land was confiscated that by the time of the English Restoration, Catholics owned less than 10 percent of the land in Ireland; they had owned 60 percent of the land in 1641.

As you can imagine, all of this further intensified the deep resentment and bitterness between the Irish and English. Anglo-Irish relations were nothing more than a series of rebellions and harsh reprisals. The English failed again and again to understand the situation in Ireland and only succeeded in maintaining control through military force. Unfortunately, this pattern was not destined to change anytime soon.

Jacobite Ireland

With the restoration of the monarchy and the ascension of Charles II, things in Ireland did look up briefly. Charles II restored some of the lands that had been taken during the Cromwellian era to the Catholics. Charles II was the first monarch in quite a while who was sympathetic to the Irish Catholics, but his sympathy only extended to not bothering them. He needed the support of the Irish Protestants, who were now the landowning class in Ireland and thus the ones who controlled the purse strings.

When James II became king in 1685, the Catholics finally had a king on their side. During the three short years of his reign, the Irish army saw an influx of Catholics, and Protestants were removed from many local government positions. The New English began to leave the country. It seemed like the tide might finally be turning to the Catholics, but then the Glorious Revolution happened.

In the Glorious Revolution, Ireland was the only one of James II's three kingdoms to stay loyal. After fleeing England, James II devised a plan, with the support of the French, where he would seize control of the Irish throne and use Ireland as a base from which to retake England. In 1689, James II landed at Kinsale and set out to do just that.

James II's takeover of Ireland initially went rather well. He had the support of the Irish Catholics, so he had control of the south and west of Ireland. Ulster in the north was the Protestant holdout, and James II's forces had them under siege. It looked like James II might be able to move on to invade England, but then King William III arrived to personally take command of the situation.

William III at the Battle of the Boyne by Jan Wyck.
https://commons.wikimedia.org/wiki/File:King_William_III_at_the_battle_of_the_Boyne,_1690.jpg

William's forces began pushing back James II's troops, and at the Battle of the Boyne on July 1st, 1690, the two sides clashed. It was the largest battle to occur in the British Isles, and James II's side was forced to retreat. Although his army was still intact, the defeat caused James II to flee back to France. He would never again set foot in the British Isles. Despite James II's flight, his army held out for another year before being defeated in 1691.

Once again, the Irish Catholics had fought in the hopes of retaking control of Ireland, and once again, they had failed. The Protestant landowners' retribution in the wake of the Battle of the Boyne and the defeat of the Irish Catholics was, to put it mildly, harsh. Over the next few decades, the Irish Parliament, which was controlled by the Protestants, passed the Penal Code, which forbade Catholics from doing practically anything, from voting to carrying a sword to buying land worth more than a certain amount.

So, as the early modern era came to a close, Ireland was in a pretty miserable position. The majority of the population were Catholic, and they had virtually no rights. The country was controlled by London, but London had no understanding of the Irish people and acted only in the interest of the English Protestant ruling class. The numerous rebellions show that the Irish question was indeed a problem for England during the early modern era, but by the end of the era, England had come no closer to solving it. If anything, it was worse than before.

Chapter 15: Conquest and Colonization

In 1919, the British Empire reached its height with territories on every continent. It took three hundred years for this small island to reach the point where it controlled an area that spanned the entire globe, and it all got started in the early modern era.

The First British Colony

So, where did it all start? What was the first settlement that began what would become the largest empire in history? Was it Plymouth? Jamestown? What about the lost colony of Roanoke or the fisheries in Newfoundland?

We tend to focus on the colonies across the Atlantic when considering the start of the British Empire, but the first colony was a lot closer to home. Remember that England conquered both Wales and Ireland in the Middle Ages. Now conquest does not necessarily equal colonization. Colonization involves creating settlements, and while England did not do that in the Middle Ages, the English did begin to colonize Ireland in the early modern period.

Although we don't often think of Ireland as being an English colony, the plantations discussed in the last chapter, where land was confiscated and redistributed to new English settlers, are a textbook example of colonization. The land was conquered and then settled to establish the dominance of the English over the original Irish population.

Although the plantations were a core part of Elizabeth I's policy, they began during Queen Mary's reign. Mary approved the creation of English plantations in Ireland during her short reign from 1553 to 1558. This makes Ireland the first English colony, and as you likely noticed from the previous chapter, it was not exactly a successful colony. Ireland constantly rebelled, costing the English lots of blood and money. The plantations themselves were not extremely successful monetarily either. If England's other colonies followed the pattern of Ireland, colonization would prove to be more difficult than it was worth.

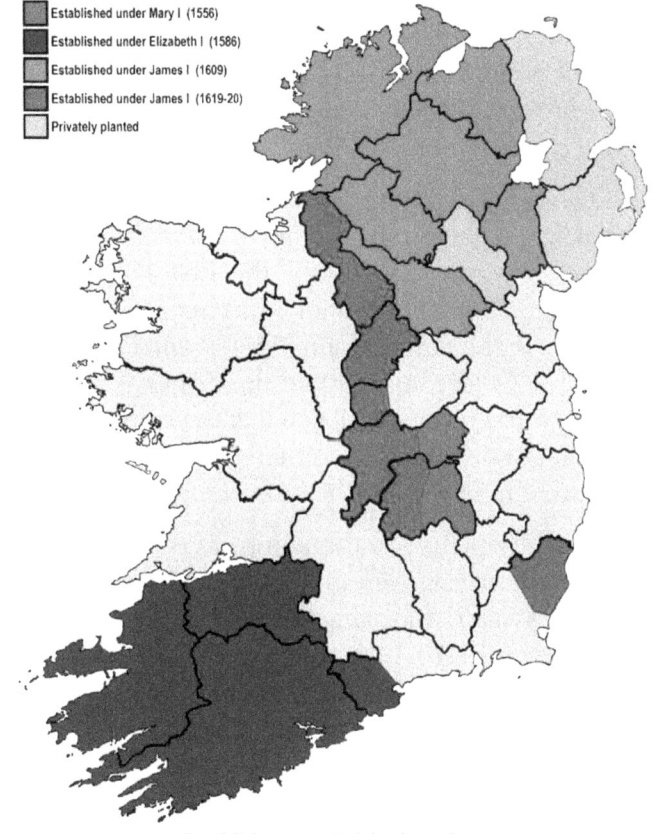

Establishment of Irish plantations.
User: Asarlaí, CC BY-SA 4.0 <https://creativecommons.org/licenses/by-sa/4.0>, via Wikimedia Commons: https://commons.wikimedia.org/wiki/File:Plantations_in_Ireland.png

Early Attempts at Colonization

Since we know what happened later, we often think of Britain as being the king of colonization, but as we mentioned in Chapter 7, England was late to the party. Spain was the first to jump on the colonization train, establishing its first settlement in 1493. The New World brought Spain vast wealth, and by the Elizabethan era, England was aware that it had missed out.

England's first attempts at colonization did not go as planned. The first area English explorers discovered was Newfoundland in 1497. Newfoundland proved to have an abundance of one particular resource: fish. Fish, however, did not require a permanent colony. English fishermen would sail over to the Newfoundland area, fill their ships with fish, and then sail back to sell the fish. Newfoundland would eventually become a colony in 1610, but for around a century, it remained a fishing outpost and not a settlement.

The next colonization attempt was an actual settlement. In 1587, Sir Walter Raleigh approved the settling of Roanoke. Had Roanoke been successful, it would have been the first English settlement across the Atlantic. However, Roanoke was not successful. The first year was difficult, so the mayor, John White, sailed back to England for more supplies. When he returned three years later, the colony was abandoned. It has been speculated that the colonists moved to a nearby island and joined the natives there, but to this day, we don't know for sure what happened to the lost colony of Roanoke.

This was the Elizabethan era's attempt at colonization. Despite the exploration and daring ventures of famous sailors like Francis Drake and Sir Walter Raleigh, England did not achieve any permanent settlements across the Atlantic. This might seem strange because we tend to connect exploration and colonization together. Explorers find new places, and then those places get colonized.

That is technically how it works, but saying it like that greatly condenses how long that takes, especially back then. Traveling across the Atlantic took weeks, and you could not set up a settlement on your first trip. Explorers like Walter Raleigh made several voyages to determine where the best place for a settlement would be. You needed to be at least somewhat familiar with the area before bringing over colonists. There were many decades between discovering the New World and settling it.

So, the wealth England gained in the grand Age of Exploration was mostly due to piracy and participation in the slave trade rather than from its settlements. The Spanish had discovered gold in the New World. So far, the English had found fish.

The Age of Colonization

In the Stuart era, colonization really kicked off for the English. The first permanent colony of Jamestown was founded in 1607, and other colonies soon followed. St. Kitts, Barbados, and Nevis (all islands in the Caribbean) were settled by the English in the 1620s. The English established trading posts in Bengal in 1636 and gained control of Bombay in 1661. In 1655, the British took Jamaica from the Spanish and then seized control of the New Netherlands (which became New York) from the Dutch in 1664. The Bahamas was colonized in 1666, and the 1713 Treaty of Utrecht (the treaty that ended the War of the Spanish Succession) gave Britain control of Hudson Bay, Newfoundland, and more.

What all those dates and place names illustrate is the gradual and steady expansion of British colonial power in the Stuart era. While the Stuarts saw a lot of internal conflict in things like the English Civil War and the Glorious Revolution, Britain's foreign power was growing. In fact, in some ways, the internal conflicts might have helped to fuel the drive for colonization.

The chaos of the English Civil War sparked the growth of several religious sects, some of which, like the Quakers, would seek religious freedom in the colonies. After the Restoration especially, England was far less friendly to the Puritans and other Dissenters (Protestants outside of the Church of England), prompting many to try their luck across the Atlantic. Colonies, such as Plymouth, Massachusetts Bay, and Pennsylvania, were founded by people seeking the freedom to practice their religion in peace.

However, saying that a lot of the British colonies were founded for freedom of religion can be potentially misleading. Ironically, the groups that traveled to the New World for religious reasons tended not to be for religious freedom in general. For instance, the Massachusetts Bay Colony (which was founded by Puritans) banished those who disagreed with their beliefs. They could do this because the governments of these colonies were often theocracies, meaning church leaders were also the government leaders. So, the idea that America has always been about religious freedom and the separation of church and state is far from the truth. Several of the first American colonies were religiously strict and theocratic.

Religion was not the only reason people moved to the colonies. The other leading factor was of a more earthly nature: economics. As we discussed in Chapter 11, poverty was a growing problem in England, and the colonies offered an opportunity for those who were down on their luck. Poor people often traveled to the colonies as indentured servants.

In theory, indentured servants had someone else pay for their passage to the colonies and then worked for that person for a certain amount of time until the debt was paid. Sometimes it did work this way, but other times, the employer of an indentured servant would add items, such as room and board, to a person's debt to ensure the person would never be able to work it off. In these circumstances, indentured servants could become virtual slaves, with their children even being forced to continue in servitude to pay off a parent's debt.

During the initial colonization of places like Virginia, indentured servants did most of the work, but this practice eventually became less popular when the colonists discovered an even cheaper source of labor: slaves. The Royal African Company was founded in 1660, and the slave trade became an integral part of American economics, particularly in the more agricultural-focused southern colonies. It would take two centuries and a very bloody war to put a stop to this horrific practice.

Indentured servants and the slave trade are a dark side of the era of colonization, and it shows just how economics-oriented colonization was. When we are young, we learn about the brave men and women who set off to lands unknown for religious freedom, adventure, and opportunity, but the fact is that most colonizers wanted to make money. The New World had resources like tobacco and sugar, and there were vast amounts of money to be made by trading those resources. Many people were abused horribly in the pursuit of that wealth.

Speaking of people who were abused in the pursuit of economic gain, there were native populations in the places the British colonized. What happened to them? The British may not have followed the practice of the Spanish conquistadors of razing native cities, but there were other ways to devastate the native populations. Smallpox was deadlier than European guns.

It is estimated that around 90 percent of the indigenous population of the Americas died from diseases brought over by the Europeans. This apocalyptic level of destruction was why the British and other Europeans were able to colonize the New World so easily. When the British colonies began to expand, they would show no hesitation about pushing the remaining natives out.

Colonization was like a fire. It provided Britain with wealth and resources, but it was destructive to many groups. Colonization is a controversial subject. There can be no doubt that the world would not exist as we know it today without the British Empire, but whether that was ultimately for the best is a question that continues to be debated.

How Did Colonization Work?

We have talked a lot about the overall shape and impact of English colonization, but now is the time to stop and consider if we know how colonization works. Is colonization just about landing somewhere, planting an English flag in the soil, and claiming the land for England? How did a place become colonized? In the following chapter, we will cover the specifics of what was happening in different English colonies in the early modern period, but let's consider the basics of the colonization process.

Although we are discussing English colonization in general, colonization was not carried out by the English government in most cases (Ireland is an exception). Instead, colonization was the work of companies.

Yes, companies. The English Crown granted charters to

companies, giving them the right to colonize and trade in certain areas. These charters gave companies a monopoly, meaning that no one else was allowed to start a settlement or trade there.

So why would a company want to start a colony? At first, they didn't. Before the founding of Jamestown in 1607, companies like the Levant Company and the East India Company were founded to trade with the Ottoman Empire and India, respectively. The Virginia Company was the first to establish a permanent settlement (Jamestown).

Founding a settlement gave a company far more control over the acquisition of resources. Without a settlement, if companies wanted to gather resources to trade, they would need to either find natives to make a deal with or only gather resources periodically, such as with fish in Newfoundland. In the case of agricultural products like tobacco and sugar, it was crucial to have settlements to farm and harvest products.

So, a company wanted to establish a colony so that it could take advantage of the resources in an area. How did it go about that? A company usually consisted of a group of wealthy individuals. Once they had the monarch's approval, which included a charter that gave them the exclusive right to trade and settle that area, this group would fund the colony. They paid for the ships and resources to send the colonists over and start the settlement. In exchange, the company had control over the resources the colony produced, as well as control over trade with the colony.

Religious colonies started in an almost identical manner. Though their goal might have been less economical, religious colonies had to request a charter from the monarch, and the owners of that charter were responsible for funding the colony. They also had control over trade in that area. Some religious groups partnered with a group of wealthy individuals to get the resources to start the settlement and agreed to give the owners so many years of the colony's profits to pay for the initial backing.

However, religious colonies made the idea of charters and companies more political by transferring the company's ownership to the colony itself. Once it had paid back its owners, the colony essentially bought back control of itself. This was what happened in

Massachusetts.

That might seem like a small difference, but it was highly significant. It made the colony an almost self-contained legal entity capable of governing itself and having only a vague connection to England. This type of independent attitude may help to explain why the American colonies were the first to rebel against British rule. New England was where many of these religious colonies were founded, and from the beginning, many of them had more of a separatist attitude toward England.

In contrast, the Caribbean colonies were almost purely economic. The sugar plantations were often owned by absentee landlords who continued to live in England, so the chances of an independence movement that stretched across class lines were virtually none. Economics was a bond that both started and strengthened colonization.

The problem with a general discussion of colonization is that it obscures the uniqueness of each situation. England colonized a lot of places. Colonization efforts in Ireland, India, the American colonies, and the Caribbean were all different. In the next chapter, we will dive deeper into the individual colonies to gain an understanding of what the British Empire looked like around the world in the early modern era.

Chapter 16: The Continuation of the Empire

In the last chapter, we looked at English colonization from a wider viewpoint. Now let's zoom in on the individual colonies for a deeper understanding of the specifics of colonization in early modern England.

The American Colonies

We are starting with the American colonies for the simple reason that England's first permanent settlement was Jamestown, Virginia, in 1607. Twelve more colonies were then founded to make the thirteen American colonies that would later become the start of the United States. Of the Thirteen Colonies, twelve were founded in the Stuart era, with the only exception being Georgia, which was founded in 1732.

Because we know that the Thirteen Colonies would later become a single nation, we often discuss them as if they were a single entity, but that was not the case. The Thirteen Colonies were thirteen separate settlements that were founded at different times and for different reasons.

Virginia was an economic venture. It was England's attempt to get a foothold in the New World. While the Jamestown settlement got off to a very rough start, it managed to survive. And when the cultivation of tobacco was introduced, it moved from surviving to thriving. By 1619, Virginia even had its own local government.

The colonies that immediately followed Virginia were less economically focused. The Pilgrims who founded Massachusetts in 1620 were Separatists (Puritans who wanted to fully separate from the Church of England). They came to the New World seeking religious freedom. Other colonies that began for religious reasons include Rhode Island (which was founded by people banished from the Massachusetts Bay Colony), Maryland (founded for Roman Catholics), and Pennsylvania (founded by the Quakers).

But economics and religion were not the only reasons colonies formed. New York and Delaware were originally founded by the Netherlands and Sweden and became English colonies when England gained control. Other later colonies were the result of population expansion and movement from the original colonies. For example, North and South Carolina were started by settlers from Virginia. The final colony, Georgia, was founded as a debtor's colony, providing a home for many of the debtors in England's prisons.

Though they may have become united later, at the start, the Thirteen Colonies were a variety pack of different groups. These were the colonies that welcomed settlers who felt uncomfortable in England for one reason or another. The colonists sought economic opportunities, religious freedom, or simply a fresh start. The fact that so many of the American colonists were looking to get away from Britain may help to explain why they were the first to rebel against British rule in 1776.

So, the American colonies were a land of opportunity for many, but just how important were they to Britain as a nation? The Thirteen Colonies were not very important economically for England. Virginia made money trading tobacco, and the southern colonies participated in the slave trade, but these colonies were not gold mines. The American colonies became almost a dumping ground for groups that Britain didn't know what to do with rather than a jewel in its colonial crown. When Britain lost the Thirteen Colonies after the American Revolutionary War, it did not put much of a dent in the British Empire's wealth. There were other colonial holdings that Britain was far more eager to hold onto.

Canada

In Canada, it was colder, which you might think meant that it was a far less profitable area, but Canada had a lot of one high-end commodity: furs.

The fur trade in the Canadian area was a lucrative business, so much so that Britain was not the only one in this area. The French had more of a presence in Canada than the British in the early modern era. It was not until Britain's victory in the Seven Years' War (1756-1763) that the French ceded control of Canada to Britain.

However, that does not mean the British were not doing anything in Canada during this time. As we mentioned in the last chapter, Newfoundland was one of the first areas that English explorers discovered in the New World in 1497. Fishermen began regularly fishing off the Canadian coast.

The first permanent English settlement in Canada was the settlement of Cupids Bay in Newfoundland in 1610. This was rather early in the history of English colonialism, coming only three years after the founding of Jamestown, but the settlement only lasted until 1628. Still, the founding of Cupids Bay shows that England was aware of and interested in Canada early on.

Canadian colonialism in the 17th century was dominated by the French. The only other major development for the English was the founding of the Hudson's Bay Company in 1670. The Hudson's Bay Company was primarily interested in the fur trade, and unlike tobacco in Virginia and sugar in the Caribbean, the easiest way to engage in the fur trade was to trade with the natives, who were far better at navigating the Canadian wilderness and trapping animals.
This meant that the Hudson's Bay Company was not nearly as interested in creating the type of permanent settlements that existed in the southern American colonies. Instead, they built trading posts from which they conducted trade with the natives. Most of these

posts were seized by the French, but the British were able to regain control as part of the Treaty of Utrecht, which ended the War of the Spanish Succession.

The Treaty of Utrecht's effect on fur trading posts in Canada shows just how connected the British Empire was. Successes in a war that largely took place on the European continent were instrumental in helping the British maintain control of Hudson's Bay. While they may have been geographically distinct from England, it is impossible to understand the history of England without considering its colonies.

The Caribbean

Speaking of colonies that had a profound impact on England, the Caribbean, or the West Indies as it was referred to at the time, were the money-making colonies. It was through sugar plantations in the West Indies that many British fortunes were made.

The West Indies, however, did not begin in British hands. By the time the English arrived on the scene, the Spanish had already seized control of most of the West Indies. The English, however, were not willing to let the wealth this tropical paradise had to offer slip through their fingers. At first, English privateers simply tried to turn a profit by selling slaves from Africa to the Spanish colonies in the Caribbean. However, the Spanish government did not want their monopoly on trade disrupted and destroyed the English vessels attempting to trade. This led to a more aggressive form of English piracy. Instead of trading with Spain, the English would simply take the bullion directly from the ships.

In the Elizabethan era, English pirates were a constant threat not only in the Spanish-controlled Caribbean but also in the Pacific Ocean. When Francis Drake circumnavigated the globe, he did so at the expense of many Spanish vessels. You may be wondering why English vessels attacking Spanish ships and stealing gold did not immediately lead to war. After all, if that happened today, Spain and England would be at war almost immediately.

During this time, there was a saying that went, "No peace beyond the line." What this meant was that past a certain point in the Atlantic Ocean, the diplomacy and peace agreements of Europe no longer held sway. There is debate as to whether there was a specific line at which this occurred, but the sentiment is correct. The New World was a frontier, and the normal rules of engagement did not apply. Even if Spain and England were at peace in Europe, they regularly crashed into each other in the Caribbean. While it may have technically been the work of English pirates, it was clear to everyone that Elizabeth I supported the privateers. Francis Drake was knighted by the queen after returning from his circumnavigation of the globe, during which he plundered quite a few Spanish ships.

Elizabeth I knighting Francis Drake from the Tavistock Monument.
Lobsterthermidor at en.wikipedia, CC0, via Wikimedia Commons:
https://commons.wikimedia.org/wiki/File:DrakeKnightedTavistockMonument.jpg

This was the Tudor presence in the West Indies. It was pirates taking bites out of Spanish power, but Spanish power was destined to decline. In the Stuart era, England began by setting up colonies on islands that were yet unclaimed, such as St. Kitts (1623), Nevis (1628), and Barbados (1627).

These Caribbean settlements were excellent for crops like tobacco and sugar, but they were not as hospitable for the settlers. Tropical diseases killed a huge portion, and many settlers who were interested in starting a new life in the New World ended up moving north to the American colonies. The high mortality rate also meant that the West Indies needed a constant influx of workers to keep the plantations running, which arrived in the form of indentured servants and then slaves. The Caribbean kept the slave trade running for close to two centuries until it was banned in 1807.

So, England had a few settlements in the Caribbean by the mid-1650s, but these colonies, like the thirteen American colonies, had all been set up as private ventures. The next question was how the English government itself could profit from these colonies, and that question was answered not by a monarch but by Oliver Cromwell. During the Interregnum, Oliver Cromwell came up with two ideas to try to take advantage of the opportunities of the New World.

The first idea was the Navigation Acts. These acts prohibited English colonies from trading with foreign powers. This was based on the idea that any trade with other countries was a loss for England. The Navigation Acts were continued after the English Restoration and remained British colonial policy for around two centuries.

Oliver Cromwell's other colonial plan was more specific to the Caribbean and more ambitious. Cromwell's Western Design was a plan to seize control of Spanish colonies in the Caribbean. This marked a huge shift in the understanding of colonialism. It was the English government, not private companies, that was doing the colonizing, and instead of settling unclaimed lands, they were taking them directly from the Spanish. For the first time, the English government was directly seeking to expand its empire.

As far as how successful the Western Design was, it could have gone much better. The English failed to capture the main Spanish colony of Hispaniola. They managed to seize Jamaica in 1655, but it would cost a good deal of trouble to maintain control of it. England actually encouraged the presence of buccaneers (pirates) to help defend Jamaica from the Spanish, but when the Spanish finally backed off, the pirates were still there. England had to spend the next several decades getting piracy in the Caribbean under control.

In the Stuart era, English control in the Caribbean gradually expanded, and these colonies became crucial to the mercantilism on which colonization was based. Mercantilism is an economic system in which the government exercises strict control over the economics of its colonies. It came from the idea that a nation must have precious metals (gold and silver). If a nation did not have mines to get those metals, then they must trade for them. For a country like England to trade for gold and silver, it relied on the raw resources it gathered from its colonies. The colonies were a source of trading materials that the mother country could use to trade for precious metals.

To ensure that the motherland always had access to these raw resources, colonies were forbidden from trading with other nations and from producing manufactured goods. They were to remain reliant on the old country so that the established trade routes would remain open and profitable.

Those established trade routes can be simplified into the triangular trade system, which connected West Africa, the Caribbean and other colonies, and Europe. Slaves from West Africa were sent to the colonies, and the colonies then sent raw resources back to Europe. It was a system that greatly benefited Europe.

What all this means is that while the Caribbean was a key component of England's trade empire, the settlements mostly churned out raw goods, particularly sugar. Many of the Caribbean plantations were owned by absentee landlords who remained in England, where they enjoyed the profits of their plantations and slave labor. Someone else oversaw the daily running of the plantation. The Caribbean was a place where the English went for a few years to make their fortunes and then returned home. It was not a place where settlers moved to start a new life. The Caribbean was disease-ridden, full of pirates, and home to a cruel slave system, but all of that was overlooked for one simple reason: it made money.

Slaves cutting sugarcane.
British Library, CC0, via Wikimedia Commons:
https://commons.wikimedia.org/wiki/File:Slaves_cutting_the_sugar_cane_-_Ten_Views_in_the_Island_of_Antigua_(1823),_plate_IV_-_BL.jpg

India

We have been focusing pretty heavily on the colonies across the Atlantic, but England did not confine its colonial endeavors to the New World. There was still much wealth and power to be had in the Old World.

In the early modern era, India was not directly colonized by Britain. Direct British control would not occur until 1858 with the establishment of the British Raj. In the early modern era, the British presence in India was largely confined to trade and was the work of a single company—the English East India Company.

The English East India Company was formed in 1600. The royal charter that created the company gave it a monopoly on trade in India, as well as Southeast and East Asia.

The English East India Company began with the spice trade. At first, each trading voyage was treated as a separate investment. Each voyage was planned and funded as its own expedition. It was not until 1657 that a permanent joint stock was created. The creation of a joint stock meant the company could make money as a whole instead of having individuals invest separately and profit separately. In other words, the company was more of a single entity.

The English East India Company may have started relatively small, but it soon grew ambitious. Trade expanded from just spices to cotton and silk. While the company attempted to trade in the area that is now Indonesia, they were pushed out by the Dutch. However, the company was able to defeat the Portuguese in India in 1612 and gain trading rights with the Mughal Empire. This development turned the company's focus from East Asia to India.

In India, with the agreement of the Mughal Empire, the English East India Company set up trading posts (known as factories). They then began to turn a nice profit, which caused other merchants in England to resent the company's monopoly. There were several attempts by other companies to seize part of the business, but none of the East India Company's competitors were able to break its monopoly. However, by the end of the early modern era, the English government insisted that the East India Company merge with its competitors to create the United Company of Merchants of England. That's a mouthful of a name, but it was basically the same company, only larger.

At this point, the English East India Company may sound like nothing more than a group of merchants peacefully trading with the natives, but there's more going on here. To ensure that their monopolies were not encroached on by other nations, many countries used force to keep the natives trading with them exclusively. In the late 17th century, the English East India Company tried to do that but found that the Mughal Empire was too strong to be coerced. Instead of securing its trading rights, the company harmed its relations with the empire and was forced to build its own trading port in Calcutta in 1690. The factories also had to be turned into forts.

This new, more violent relationship with India would eventually transform the English East India Company from a group of merchants interested in trade into an entity on par with a government. The company had its own army. It could make treaties, ally itself with different groups, and levy taxes. The English East India Company was private colonization at its most extreme, but this colonization was purely economic. The English were not interested in settling in India. Like the Caribbean, the main purpose of England's presence in India was to make money.

By 1714 and the end of the early modern era, the British Empire was steadily growing. Most of Britain's colonies were for economic gain, and the wealth these colonies provided would allow Britain to defend and expand its empire over the next two hundred years. England had come out of the medieval age war-torn and chaotic after the Wars of the Roses. It ended the early modern age with a growing empire. Britain was a world power.

Conclusion

A lot happened in early modern England. Wars (both internal and external), religious changes, the Renaissance, new discoveries, and changing economics all contributed to transforming England during this time.

Looking at each of these aspects separately has allowed us to gain a broad view of what happened in early modern England, but we should also remember that these events did not happen in isolation. In a book, it is easy to separate discussions of religious changes, colonization, and social structure, but in reality, all of these things are deeply intertwined.

Take the execution of Mary, Queen of Scots, for example. This one event was impacted by many of the larger trends going on. Mary was kicked out of Scotland and took shelter in England. Although she was politically Elizabeth I's enemy, refusing shelter to a fellow monarch would have upset the idea of the Great Chain of Being, at least in Elizabeth's eyes. Monarchs had to stick together, or else they jeopardized the very idea of monarchy.

However, this put Elizabeth I in a dilemma. Mary, Queen of Scots was a Catholic and the next in line for the English throne. That made her a natural rallying point for the Catholics in England, who were still hoping to reverse the Reformation. Then there was also the problem of the Spanish. England and Spain were in conflict over English piracy and the Netherlands, and Mary, Queen of Scots was an easy way for the Spanish to sow plots and hopefully destabilize the English court.

Thus, when Elizabeth I decided to execute her cousin, it was fueled by several factors. Mary was a problem for both England's foreign affairs and internal religious peace. However, Elizabeth I still needed to demonstrate a belief in the Great Chain of Being. Chopping off a fellow monarch's head disrupted the idea that monarchs were divinely appointed. So, what did Elizabeth I do?

Elizabeth I signed Mary's death warrant but did not order the warrant to be sent to the Tower to be carried out. Her secretary, William Davison, sent the warrant without her explicit orders. Mary, who had been a thorn in Elizabeth I's side, was out of the way, but Elizabeth was able to claim that she had not ordered her death. Davison took the fall and was arrested and imprisoned. However, he was soon released quietly, leading most people to assume that it was all part of Elizabeth's plan.

This event shows us a glimpse of how all the different areas of early modern England combined to shape the country in this era. The decision to execute Mary arose out of religious tensions, foreign conflict, and also plain politics.

The execution of Mary, Queen of Scots is far from the only event to be so multi-faceted. The Glorious Revolution was the final rejection of Catholicism and also demonstrated how the ideology of the Great Chain of Being was collapsing. The break with the Roman Catholic Church was only made possible by the wider religious changes in Europe, but it was brought about largely for political reasons, namely Henry VIII's desperation for a male heir. We place these events in categories, but the reality is more often a mixture of factors.

The larger trends that create these events are intertwined as well. Trade not only boosted the national economy overall but also brought more relative stability to an economy that was previously solely agricultural and, therefore, subject to the mood of the weather. The importance of trade pushed England to want a piece of the colonization pie, especially when England's main export, wool, began to stagnate. England's empire-building led to conflicts with foreign nations, and England's success in those conflicts is what allowed it to continue building its empire.

The Reformation is another movement whose impact went beyond religion. The dissolution of the monasteries forced England to come up with another way to care for the poor, and the growing poor prompted many people to move to the New World. The failure to convert Ireland to the new religion would lead to increasing tensions between England and Ireland. The conflict with Ireland pushed England over the final edge into civil war. The Reformation also sparked a growing fear of popery, which eventually led to the Glorious Revolution.

The point is that it is all connected. We can study early modern England from the perspective of religion, politics, social structure, foreign affairs, and more, but we should never lose sight of the fact that all of these aspects are part of a single story. Early modern England was a time of great change. It saw religious transformation, the beginning of an empire, the centralization of government, the growth of Parliament's power, the decline of the monarchy, the increasing wealth of the rich alongside a growing poor class, the rise in education and professional careers, and much more.

All of those changes combined to transform England from a medieval society to the beginnings of the modern society we know today. The period from 1485 to 1714 was the start of a new direction for England and the world, so, in many ways, it does deserve the name of *early modern* England.

Here's another book by Enthralling History that you might like

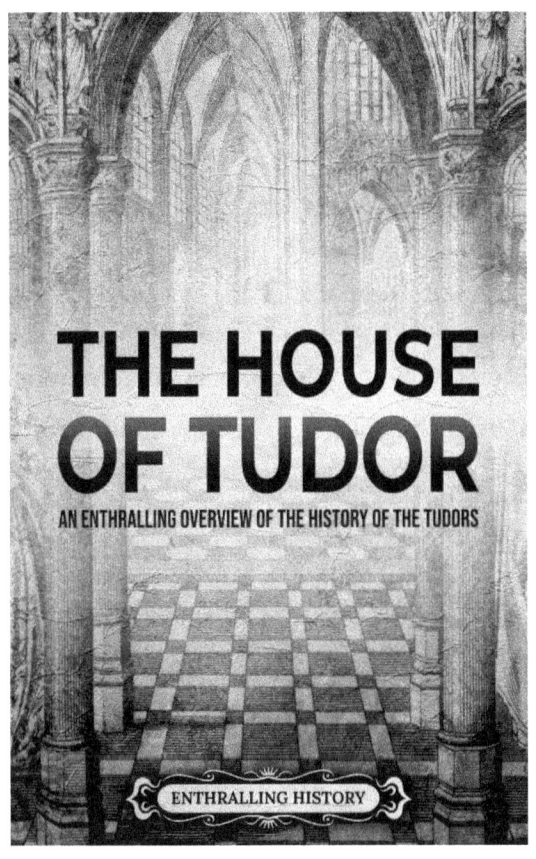

Free limited time bonus

Stop for a moment. We have a free bonus set up for you. The problem is this: we forget 90% of everything that we read after 7 days. Crazy fact, right? Here's the solution: we've created a printable, 1-page pdf summary for this book that you're reading now. All you have to do to get your free pdf summary is to go to the following website: **https://livetolearn.lpages.co/enthrallinghistory/**

Once you do, it will be intuitive. Enjoy, and thank you!

Bibliography

"13 Colonies: Facts, Information, Colonies & History." Revolutionary War, March 4, 2020. https://www.revolutionary-war.net/13-colonies/.

Admin. "Shakespeare's Works." Shakespeare's Works. Folger Shakespeare Library, April 3, 2020. https://www.folger.edu/shakespeares-works.

Ashley, M. and Morrill, John S. "Oliver Cromwell." Encyclopedia Britannica, August 30, 2021. https://www.britannica.com/biography/Oliver-Cromwell.

Bowen, Lloyd. "Information, Language and Political Culture in Early Modern Wales." Past & Present, no. 228 (August 1, 2015): 125–58. https://search.ebscohost.com/login.aspx?direct=true&AuthType=ip,shib&db=edsjsr&AN=edsjsr.24544897&site=eds-live&scope=site.

Bradford, E. and Fernández-Armesto, Felipe. "Sir Francis Drake." Encyclopedia Britannica, January 24, 2022. https://www.britannica.com/biography/Francis-Drake.

Brain, Jessica. "Timeline of the British Empire." Historic UK, February 8, 2019. https://www.historic-uk.com/HistoryUK/HistoryofBritain/Timeline-Of-The-British-Empire/.

Brain, Jessica. "Titus Oates and the Popish Plot." Historic UK. Accessed May 25, 2022. https://www.historic-uk.com/HistoryUK/HistoryofEngland/Titus-Oates-Popish-Plot/.

Britannica, T. Editors of Encyclopedia. "American Colonies." Encyclopedia Britannica, October 19, 2021. https://www.britannica.com/topic/American-colonies.

Britannica, T. Editors of Encyclopedia. "Anglo-Dutch Wars." Encyclopedia Britannica, December 13, 2021. https://www.britannica.com/event/Anglo-Dutch-Wars.

Britannica, T. Editors of Encyclopedia. "Anne." Encyclopedia Britannica, February 2, 2022. https://www.britannica.com/biography/Anne-queen-of-Great-Britain-and-Ireland.

Britannica, T. Editors of Encyclopedia. "Book of Sports." Encyclopedia Britannicà, February 14, 2022. https://www.britannica.com/topic/Book-of-Sports.

Britannica, T. Editors of Encyclopedia. "British Empire." Encyclopedia Britannica, March 13, 2022. https://www.britannica.com/place/British-Empire.

Britannica, T. Editors of Encyclopedia. "Clarendon Code." Encyclopedia Britannica, March 3, 2021. https://www.britannica.com/event/Clarendon-Code.

Britannica, T. Editors of Encyclopedia. "East India Company." Encyclopedia Britannica, February 12, 2021. https://www.britannica.com/topic/East-India-Company.

Britannica, T. Editors of Encyclopedia. "Great Chain of Being." Encyclopedia Britannica, December 10, 2021. https://www.britannica.com/topic/Great-Chain-of-Being.

Britannica, T. Editors of Encyclopedia. "Gunpowder Plot." Encyclopedia Britannica, December 13, 2021. https://www.britannica.com/event/Gunpowder-Plot.

Britannica, T. Editors of Encyclopedia. "Hudson's Bay Company." Encyclopedia Britannica, May 7, 2020. https://www.britannica.com/topic/Hudsons-Bay-Company.

Britannica, T. Editors of Encyclopedia. "King James Version." Encyclopedia Britannica, February 2, 2021. https://www.britannica.com/topic/King-James-Version.

Britannica, T. Editors of Encyclopedia. "Mary II." Encyclopedia Britannica, December 24, 2021. https://www.britannica.com/biography/Mary-II.

Britannica, T. Editors of Encyclopedia. "Massachusetts Bay Colony." Encyclopedia Britannica, June 6, 2021. https://www.britannica.com/place/Massachusetts-Bay-Colony.

Britannica, T. Editors of Encyclopedia. "Mercantilism." Encyclopedia Britannica, May 13, 2020. https://www.britannica.com/topic/mercantilism.

Britannica, T. Editors of Encyclopedia. "Peerage." Encyclopedia Britannica, September 6, 2019. https://www.britannica.com/topic/peerage.

Britannica, T. Editors of Encyclopedia. "Poor Law." Encyclopedia Britannica, May 19, 2020. https://www.britannica.com/event/Poor-Law.

Britannica, T. Editors of Encyclopedia. "Printing Press." Encyclopedia Britannica, October 1, 2021. https://www.britannica.com/technology/printing-press.

Britannica, T. Editors of Encyclopedia. "Puritanism." Encyclopedia Britannica, May 15, 2020. https://www.britannica.com/topic/Puritanism.

Britannica, T. Editors of Encyclopedia. "Renaissance." Encyclopedia Britannica, March 30, 2022. https://www.britannica.com/event/Renaissance.

Britannica, T. Editors of Encyclopedia. "Short Parliament." I, June 23, 2019. https://www.britannica.com/topic/Short-Parliament.

Britannica, T. Editors of Encyclopedia. "Southwark." Encyclopedia Britannica, April 10, 2014. https://www.britannica.com/place/Southwark-London.

Britannica, T. Editors of Encyclopedia. "Spanish Armada." Encyclopedia Britannica, February 5, 2021. https://www.britannica.com/topic/Armada-Spanish-naval-fleet.

Britannica, T. Editors of Encyclopedia. "Toleration Act." Encyclopedia Britannica, May 17, 2022. https://www.britannica.com/event/Toleration-Act-Great-Britain-1689.

Britannica, T. Editors of Encyclopedia. "War of the Grand Alliance." Encyclopedia Britannica, December 13, 2016. https://www.britannica.com/event/War-of-the-Grand-Alliance.

Britannica, T. Editors of Encyclopedia. "War of the Spanish Succession." Encyclopedia Britannica, February 26, 2021. https://www.britannica.com/event/War-of-the-Spanish-Succession.

Bucholz, Robert, and Newton Key. Early Modern England 1485-1714: A Narrative History. 2nd ed. Chichester, West Sussex: Wiley-Blackwell, 2009.

Burton, I. F. "John Churchill, 1st Duke of Marlborough." Encyclopedia Britannica, June 14, 2021. https://www.britannica.com/biography/John-Churchill-1st-duke-of-Marlborough.

Carter, H., Gruffudd Pyrs, and Smith, Beverley. "Wales." Encyclopedia Britannica, November 30, 2021. https://www.britannica.com/place/Wales.

Castelow, Ellen. "The Pendle Witches." Historic UK. Accessed May 26, 2022. https://www.historic-uk.com/CultureUK/The-Pendle-Witches/.

Clark, James. The Dissolution of the Monasteries: A New History. New Haven: Yale University Press, 2021. https://search.ebscohost.com/login.aspx?direct=true&AuthType=ip,shib&db=nlebk&AN=3047017&site=eds-live&scope=site.

Clarke, C. Graham and Brereton, Bridget M. "West Indies." Encyclopedia Britannica, May 26, 2022. https://www.britannica.com/place/West-Indies-island-group-Atlantic-Ocean.

"Colonization." The Canadian Encyclopedia. Accessed June 14, 2022. https://www.thecanadianencyclopedia.ca/en/timeline/colonization-and-immigration.

Coops, Oliver. "Cornish Rebellion of 1497." Historic UK. Accessed May 31, 2022. https://www.historic-uk.com/HistoryUK/HistoryofEngland/Cornish-Rebellion-1497/.

Crowther, David. "Robert Kett's Petition, 1549." The History of England, May 27, 2020. https://thehistoryofengland.co.uk/resource/robert-ketts-petition-1549/.

Dickson, Andrew. "Key Features of Renaissance Culture." British Library, March 30, 2017. https://www.bl.uk/shakespeare/articles/key-features-of-renaissance-culture.

Dikshit, K., Schwartzberg, Joseph E., Srivastava, A. L., Spear, T. G. Percival, Wolpert, Stanley A., Thapar, Romila, Calkins, Philip B., Alam, Muzaffar, Subrahmanyam, Sanjay, Champakalakshmi, R., and Allchin, Frank Raymond. "India." Encyclopedia Britannica, June 8, 2022. https://www.britannica.com/place/India.

"Divine Right of Kings." Divine Right of Kings - New World Encyclopedia. Accessed February 15, 2022. https://www.newworldencyclopedia.org/entry/Divine_Right_of_Kings.

Edwards, R. Walter Dudley, Boland, Frederick Henry, Kay, Sean, Fanning, Ronan and Ranelagh, John O'Beirne. "Ireland." Encyclopedia Britannica, June 8, 2022. https://www.britannica.com/place/Ireland.

Elton, G. R., and Morrill, John S. "Henry VIII." Encyclopedia Britannica, January 24, 2022. https://www.britannica.com/biography/Henry-VIII-king-of-England

Fraser, A. "Mary." Encyclopedia Britannica, February 4, 2022. https://www.britannica.com/biography/Mary-queen-of-Scotland.

Grant, R. "Raid on the Medway." Encyclopedia Britannica, June 5, 2021. https://www.britannica.com/event/Raid-on-the-Medway.

Harris, L. and Hiller, James. "Newfoundland and Labrador." Encyclopedia Britannica, April 6, 2021. https://www.britannica.com/place/Newfoundland-and-Labrador.

Heisch, Allison. "Queen Elizabeth I: Parliamentary Rhetoric and the Exercise of Power." Signs 1, no. 1 (1975): 31–55. http://www.jstor.org/stable/3172965.

Heydenreich, L. Heinrich. "Leonardo da Vinci." Encyclopedia Britannica, April 28, 2022. https://www.britannica.com/biography/Leonardo-da-Vinci.

Hiller, J. and Harris, Leslie. "Newfoundland and Labrador." Encyclopedia Britannica, April 6, 2021. https://www.britannica.com/place/Newfoundland-and-Labrador.

Hogeback, J. "The Lost Colony of Roanoke." Encyclopedia Britannica, June 13, 2022. https://www.britannica.com/story/the-lost-colony-of-roanoke.

Johnson, Ben. "Dissolution of the Monasteries." Historic UK. Accessed May 24, 2022. https://www.historic-uk.com/HistoryUK/HistoryofEngland/Dissolution-of-the-Monasteries/.

Kenyon, J. P. "James II." Encyclopedia Britannica, October 10, 2021. https://www.britannica.com/biography/James-II-king-of-England-Scotland-and-Ireland.

Lewis, A. D. E., Glendon, Mary Ann and Kiralfy, Albert Roland. "Common Law." Encyclopedia Britannica, October 30, 2020. https://www.britannica.com/topic/common-law.

Macleod, I. C., Cameron, Ewen A., Brown, Alice and Moulton, Matthew James. "Scotland." Encyclopedia Britannica, October 6, 2021. https://www.britannica.com/place/Scotland.

Marty, M. E., Bainton, Roland H., Spalding, James C., Nelson, E. Clifford and Chadwick, W. Owen. "Protestantism." Encyclopedia Britannica, March 7, 2022. https://www.britannica.com/topic/Protestantism.

Mattingly, Garrett. "No Peace Beyond What Line?" Transactions of the Royal Historical Society 13 (1963): 145–62. https://doi.org/10.2307/3678733.

Mathew, D. "James I." Encyclopedia Britannica, June 15, 2021. https://www.britannica.com/biography/James-I-king-of-England-and-Scotland.

McMullan, John L. "CRIME, LAW AND ORDER IN EARLY MODERN ENGLAND." The British Journal of Criminology 27, no. 3 (1987): 252–74. http://www.jstor.org/stable/23637302.

Meigs, Samantha A., and Stanford E. Lehmberg. The Peoples of the British Isles: A New History: From Prehistoric Times to 1688. 4th ed. New York: Oxford University Press, 2016.

Mills, G. E.M. and Momsen, Janet D. "Saint Kitts and Nevis." Encyclopedia Britannica, March 10, 2021. https://www.britannica.com/place/Saint-Kitts-and-Nevis.

Morrill, J. S. "Edward Hyde, 1st Earl of Clarendon." Encyclopedia Britannica, February 14, 2022. https://www.britannica.com/biography/Edward-Hyde-1st-Earl-of-Clarendon.

Morrill, J. S. "Edward VI." Encyclopedia Britannica, October 8, 2021. https://www.britannica.com/biography/Edward-VI.

Morrill, J. S. and Greenblatt, Stephen J. "Elizabeth I." Encyclopedia Britannica, March 20, 2022. https://www.britannica.com/biography/Elizabeth-I.

Myers, A. Reginald and Morrill, John S. "Henry VII." Encyclopedia Britannica, January 24, 2022. https://www.britannica.com/biography/Henry-VII-king-of-England.

Ohlmeyer, J. H. "English Civil Wars." Encyclopedia Britannica, November 30, 2021. https://www.britannica.com/event/English-Civil-Wars.

Ravenhill, W., Barr, Nicholas A., Colley, Linda J., Gilbert, Bentley Brinkerhoff, Frere, Sheppard Sunderland, Chaney, William A., Spencer, Ulric M., Josephson, Paul R., Kellner, Peter, Hastings, Margaret, Kishlansky, Mark A., Joyce, Patrick, Briggs, Asa, Whitelock, Dorothy, Smith, Lacey Baldwin, Prestwich, Michael Charles, Morrill, John S. and Atkins, Ralph Charles. "United Kingdom." Encyclopedia Britannica, June 7, 2022. https://www.britannica.com/place/United-Kingdom.

Roseveare, H. Godfrey. "Charles II." Encyclopedia Britannica, February 2, 2022. https://www.britannica.com/biography/Charles-II-king-of-Great-Britain-and-Ireland.

Simons, E. Norman. "Mary I." Encyclopedia Britannica, February 14, 2022. https://www.britannica.com/biography/Mary-I.

Spencer, T. John Bew, Brown, John Russell and Bevington, David. "William Shakespeare." Encyclopedia Britannica, December 17, 2021. https://www.britannica.com/biography/William-Shakespeare.

Stone, Lawrence. 1949. "Elizabethan Overseas Trade." The Economic History Review 2 (1): 30–58. doi:10.2307/2590080.

Stuart, Charles I. THE KINGS SPEECH To both Houses of Parliament, the fifth of July, 1641; Ann Arbor: Text Creation Partnership, 2022. https://quod.lib.umich.edu/e/eebo/A32124.0001.001/1:2?rgn=div1;view=fulltext.

"The British West Indies." The British Empire in The Caribbean: The British West Indies. Accessed June 14, 2022. https://www.britishempire.co.uk/maproom/caribbean.htm.

"The Thirteen American Colonies." We the People. Accessed June 13, 2022. https://wethepeople.scholastic.com/grade-4-6/thirteen-american-colonies.html.

"Witchcraft - UK Parliament." UK Parliament. Accessed May 26, 2022. https://www.parliament.uk/about/living-heritage/transformingsociety/private-lives/religion/overview/witchcraft/.

Wolfe, Brendan. "Roanoke Colonies, The." Encyclopedia Virginia, May 24, 2022. https://encyclopediavirginia.org/entries/roanoke-colonies-the/.